Christmas Carols

We Wish You a
Harley Christmas

By Daniel Kibblesmith

CHRONICLE BOOKS
SAN FRANCISCO

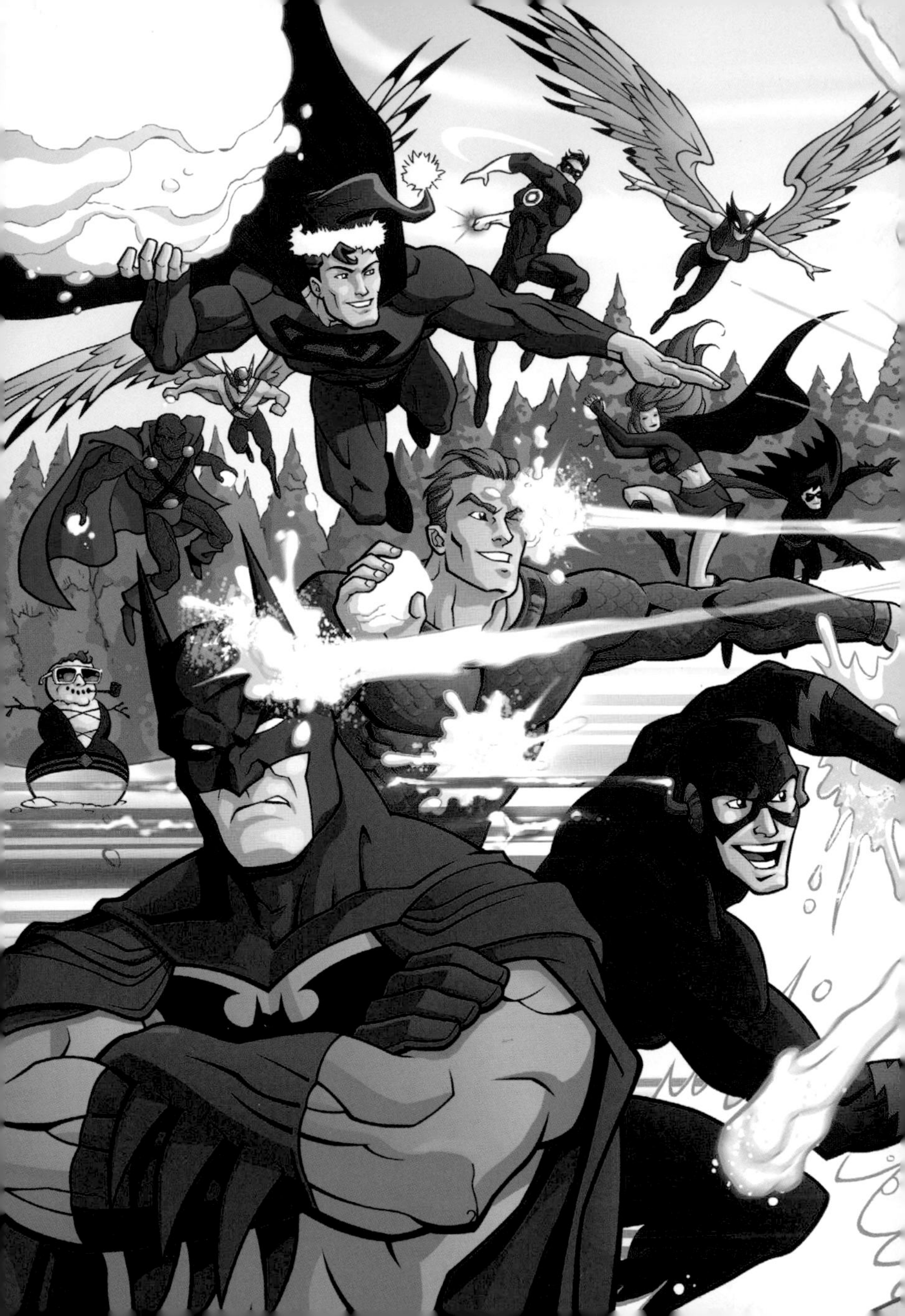

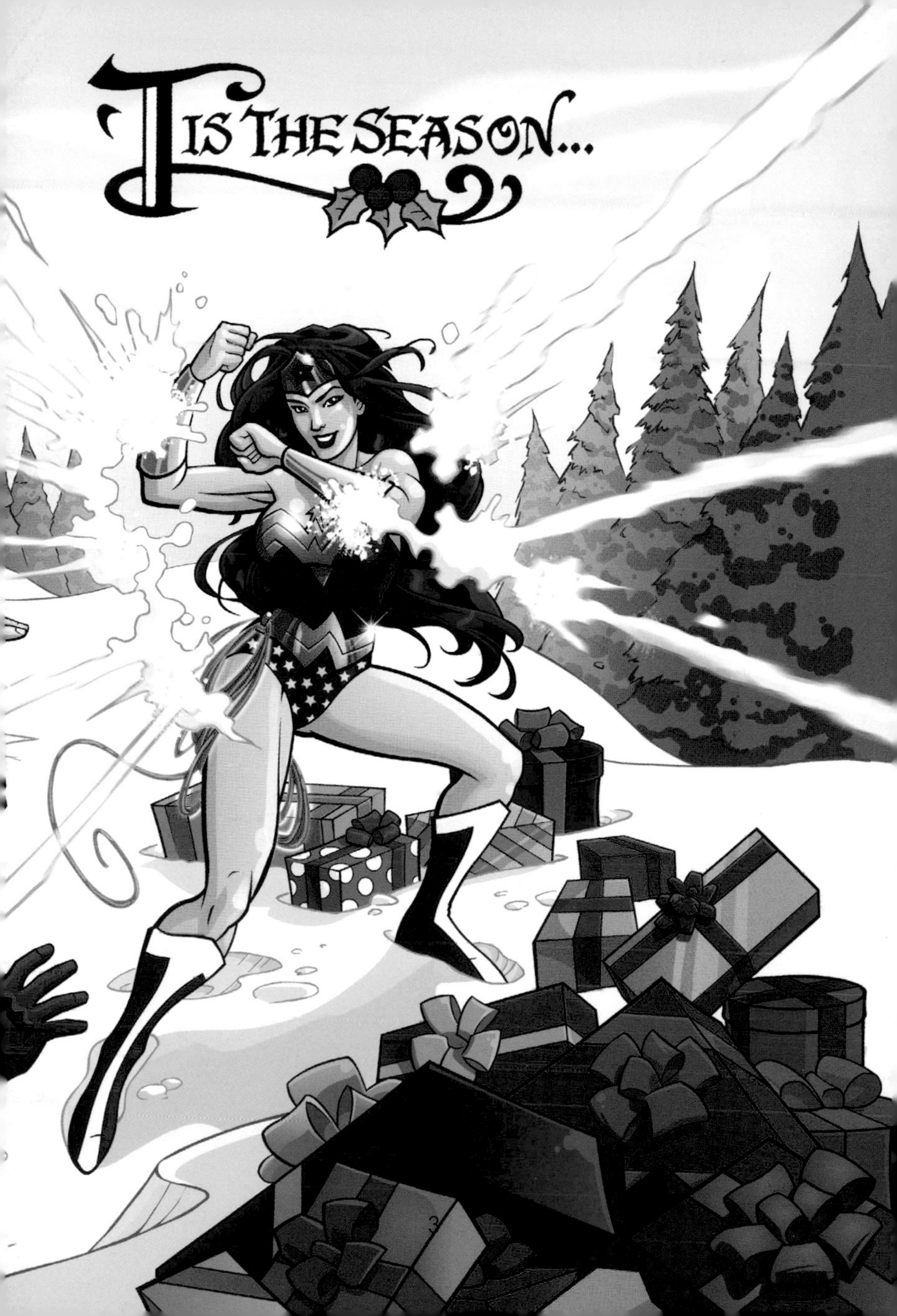
'TIS THE SEASON...

Contents

WE WISH YOU A HARLEY CHRISTMAS

"We Wish You a Merry Christmas"

We wish you a Harley Christmas
We wish you a Harley Christmas
We wish you a Harley Christmas
And a Laughing New Year

Hyenas we bring, to growl at your kin
Hyenas get hungry so make snacks appear!

They won't go until they get some
They won't go until they get some
They won't go until they get some
So bring them right here!

I'm serious, kiddos, you don't wanna end up
being the snack.

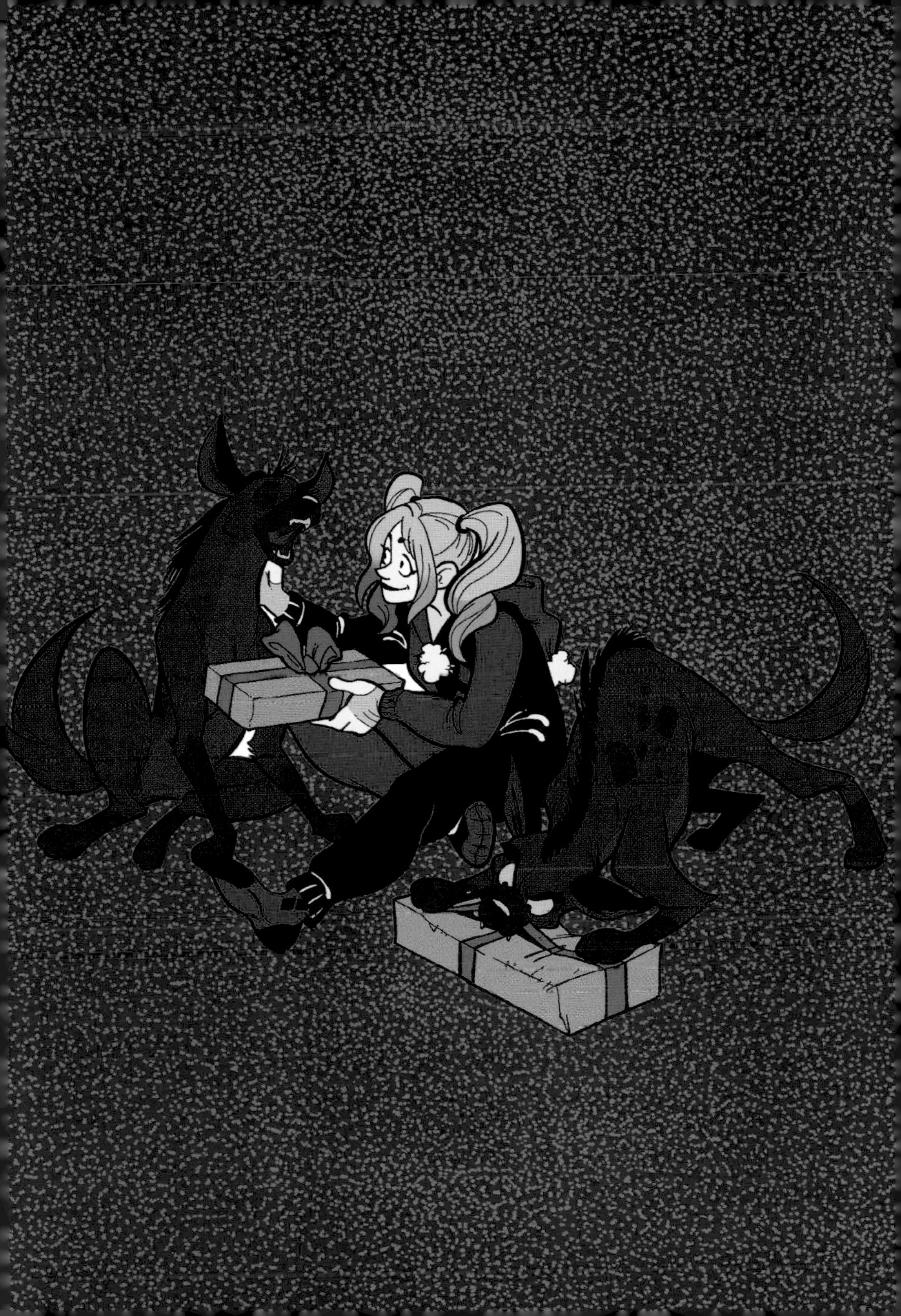

SILENT KNIGHT

"Silent Night"

Silent Knight, Gotham's Knight
Gordon's call, signal's light
Caped Crusader so valiant and wise
On his courage, all Gotham relies
Into action he leaps!
Into action he leaps!

Silent Knight, Fearless Knight
Criminals quake with fright
From above us, he watches and waits
Gliding down with unnatural grace
Evil-doers be warned!
Evil-doers be warned!

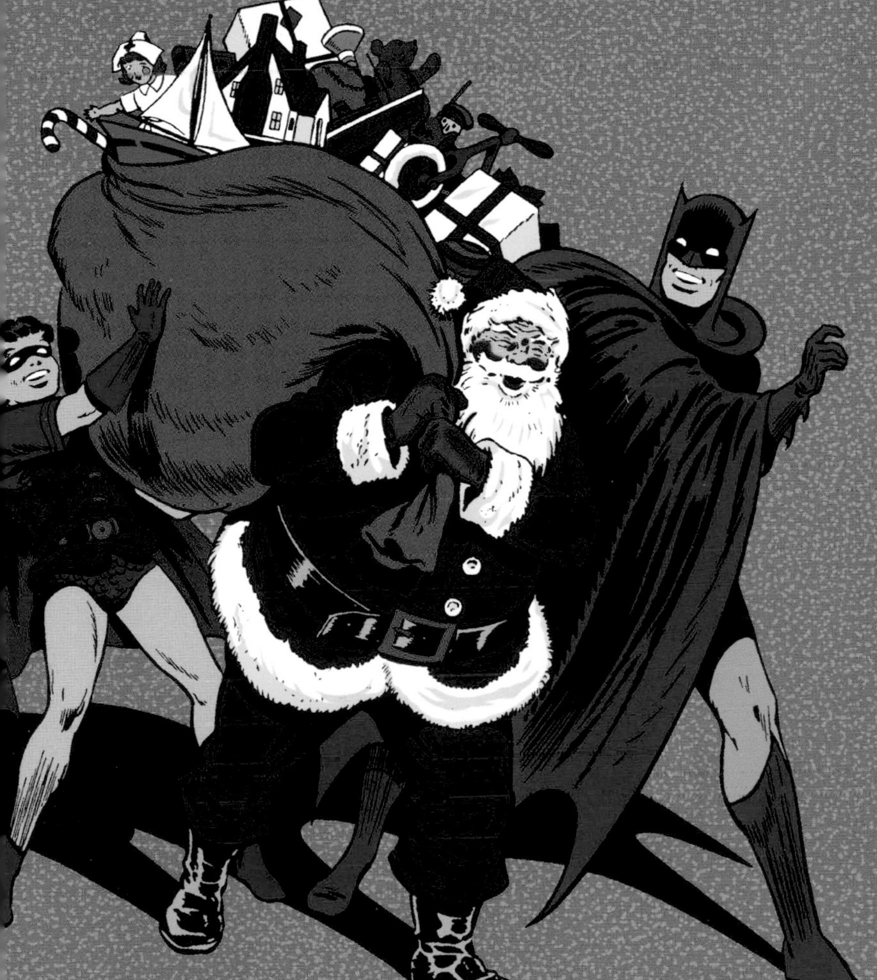

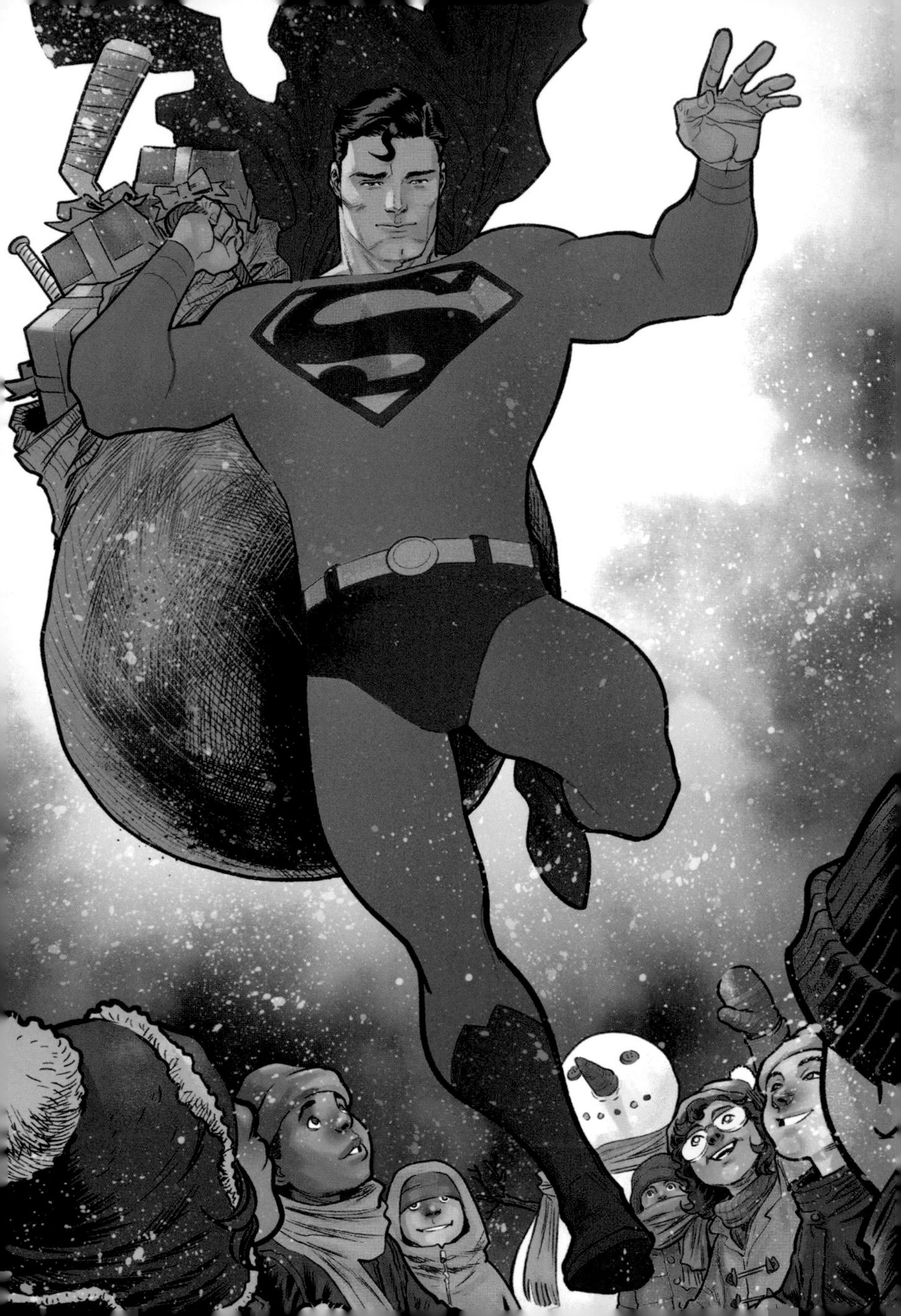

KAL-EL, KAL-EL

"The First Noel"

Around a red sun, your planet did spin
They built you a rocket and placed you within
Through the coldness of space, you journeyed so far
The hope of your race in a small shooting star

Kal-El, Kal-El
Kal-El, Kal-El
Last Son of Krypton and son of Jor-El

In fields where you landed, a couple did find
A mysterious craft with a baby inside
Under bright yellow sun, your power it grew
A symbol of hope wrapped in bright red and blue

Kal-El, Kal-El
Kal-El, Kal-El
Born is a hero who loves us so well

SILVER BANDS

"Silver Bells"

Silver bands
Silver bands
Don't commit crime in her city

KLANG! PTANG!
Bracelets rang!
Wonder Woman's on her way!

City sidewalks, shady sidewalks
Where the criminals spree
In the air there's a feeling
of Wonder

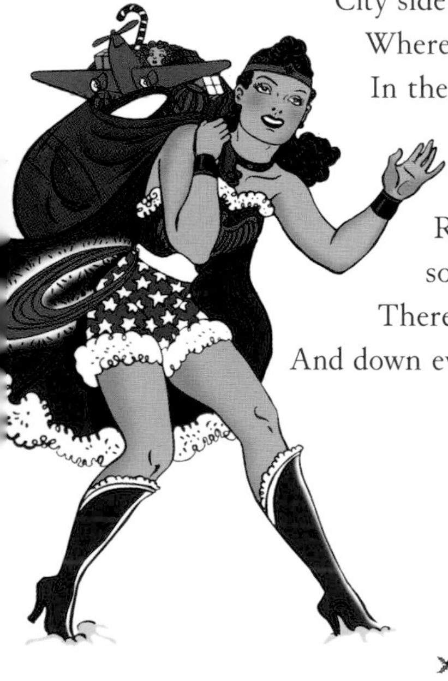

Robbers racing,
someone chasing
There is nowhere to flee
And down every dark alley, you'll hear

Silver bands
Silver bands
Don't commit crime in her city

KLANG! PTANG!
Bracelets rang!
Wonder Woman's on her way!

There's no caper that escapes her
Feel the lasso of truth
As she whips it around the lawbreakers
Each confession is a lesson
From the Amazon sleuth
And a sound that they'll never unhear

Silver bands
Silver bands
You might do time in her city

WHAM! KABLAM!
Bracelets SLAM!
Diana's saving the day

BARRY THE RED-SUIT SPEEDSTER

"Rudolph the Red-Nosed Reindeer"

Barry the red-suit speedster
Ran to places in a FLASH!
At the first sign of trouble
You should see the way he'd dash

All of the city's villains
Tried to freeze him in his tracks
When they went ROGUE together
He would face their grim attacks

Then one Central City day
Townsfolk came to say
"Flash, our hero swift and true
This whole world depends on you!"

So Barry got promoted
And turbocharged his Super-Speed
Now he protects the planet
As part of the Justice League!

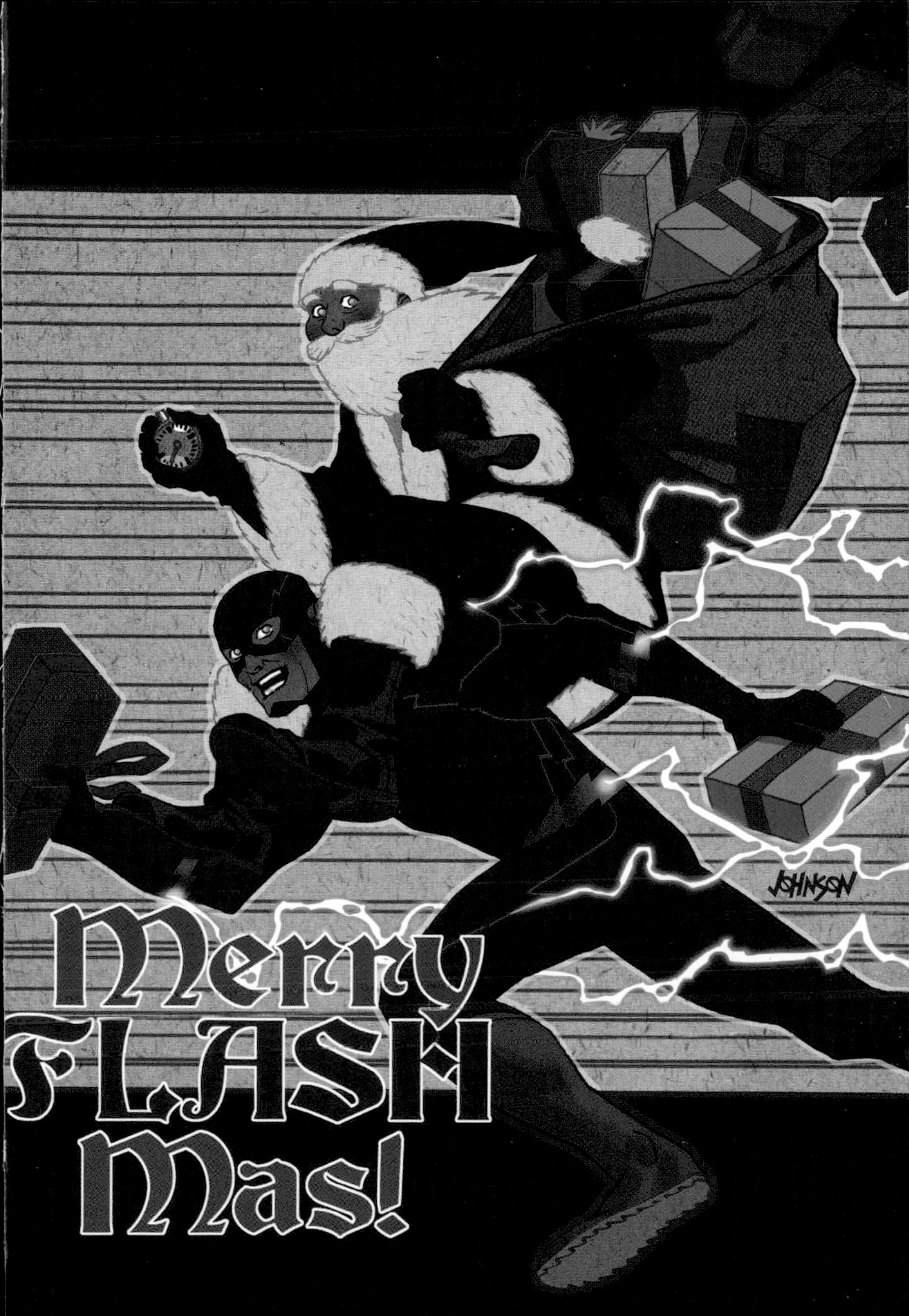
JOHNSON
Merry
FLASH
Mas!

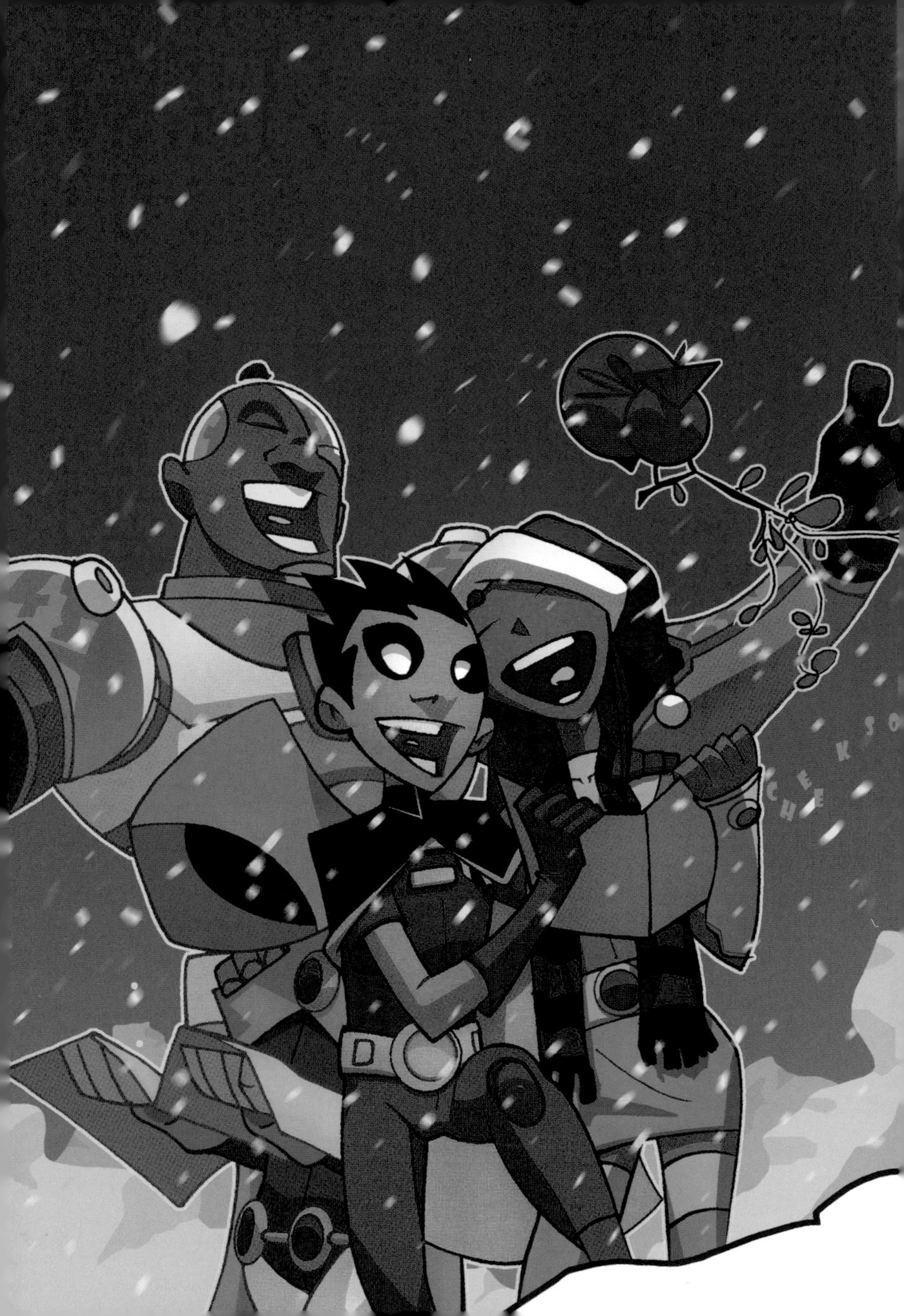

O MOTHER BOX

"O Christmas Tree"

O Mother Box, O Mother Box
The Cyborg's greatest mystery
O Mother Box, O Mother Box
The Cyborg's greatest mystery

How beautiful your circuity
When integrated into me
O Mother Box, O Mother Box
How secret is your history

O Mother Box, O Mother Box
The Cyborg's greatest mystery
O Mother Box, O Mother Box
The Cyborg's greatest mystery

You hold the power of the Source
Highfather's greatest cosmic force
O Mother Box, O Mother Box
You truly do complete me

GOOD KING AQUAMAN

"Good King Wenceslas"

Good King Aquaman looked out
On his ocean kingdom
There he spied a netted trout
Struggling for its freedom
"Won't you save me, Aquaman?!
It's my Christmas wish!"
In a single-second span,
He bravely freed the fish

Once the fish was finally free
They got down to business
"Tell me, creature of my sea,
Who or what is Christmas?"
So the fish regaled the king
With tales of yuletide days
Now each year he celebrates
Underneath the waves

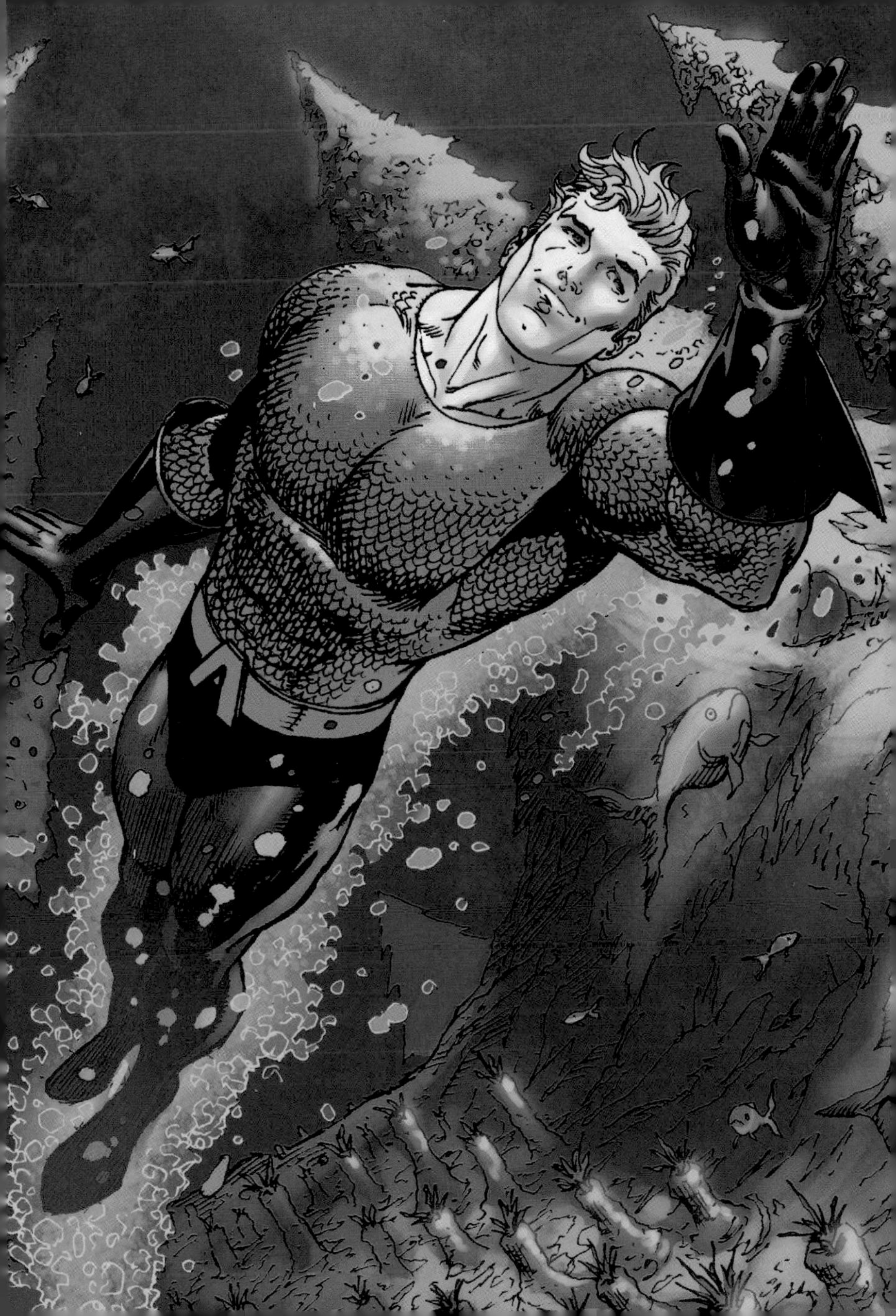

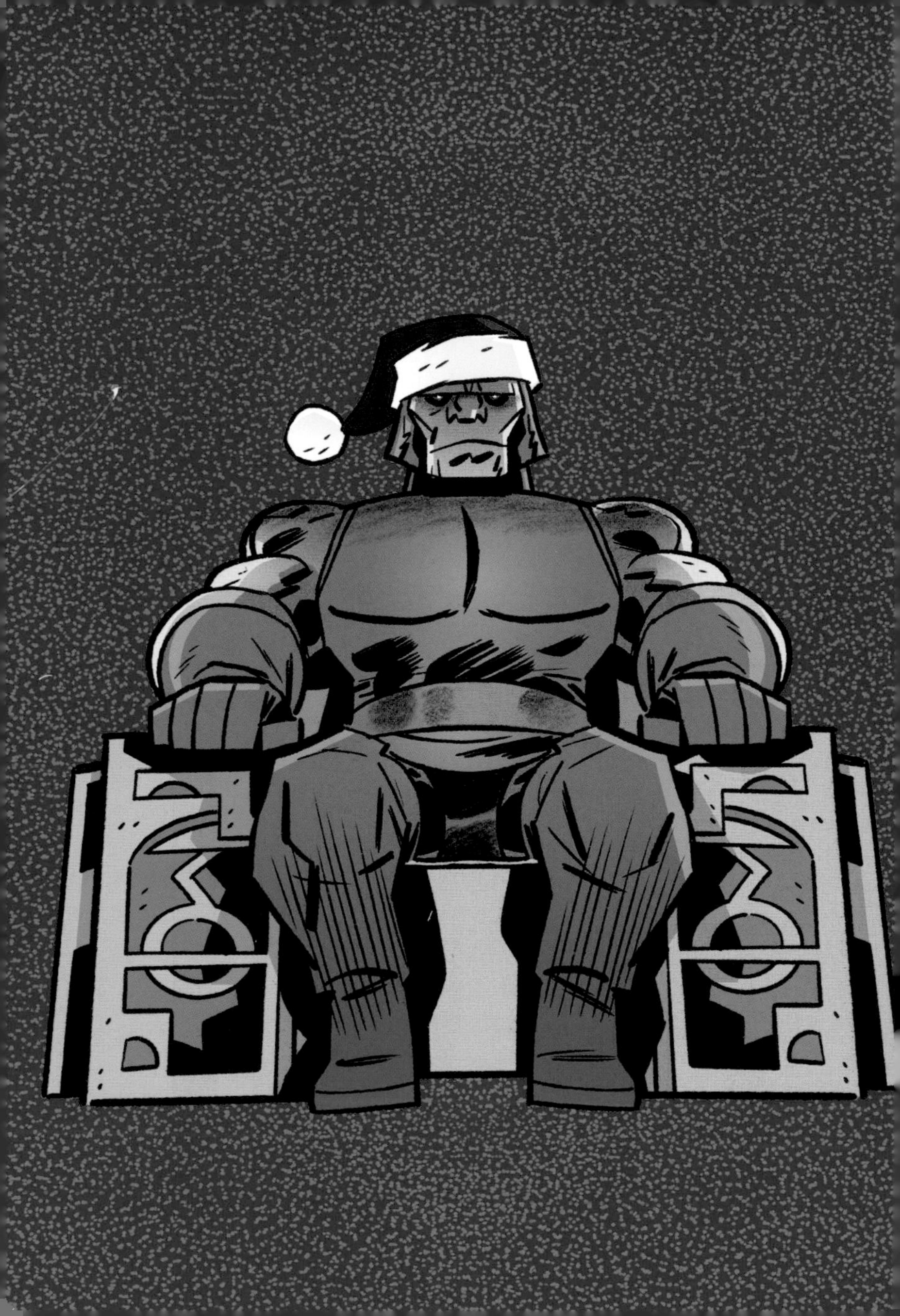

HARK THE PARADEMONS SING

"Hark the Herald Angels Sing"

Hark the Parademons sing
Glory to their planet's king!
On the world Apokolips
All must hail that DARKSEID IS

Fearful all ye subjects scream
At his grave Omega Beam
With eternal toil and strife
Praise his quest for Anti-Life
Heroes of New Genesis
Cower in fear–for DARKSEID IS!

J'ONN J'ONZZ
THE MARTIAN

"Frosty the Snowman"

J'onn J'onzz the Martian
Was a hero through and through
With heroic strength he'd go any length
In protecting me and you

J'onn J'onzz the Martian
Was the last one of his kind
And he flew and phased and shot "Martian rays"
When he wasn't reading minds

There must have been some magic
In that iron red Martian dirt
To power his heroic feats
When he joined us here on Earth

J'onn J'onzz the Martian
Never tires or fatigues
Though his fear is fire, he will never perspire
Fighting with the Justice League

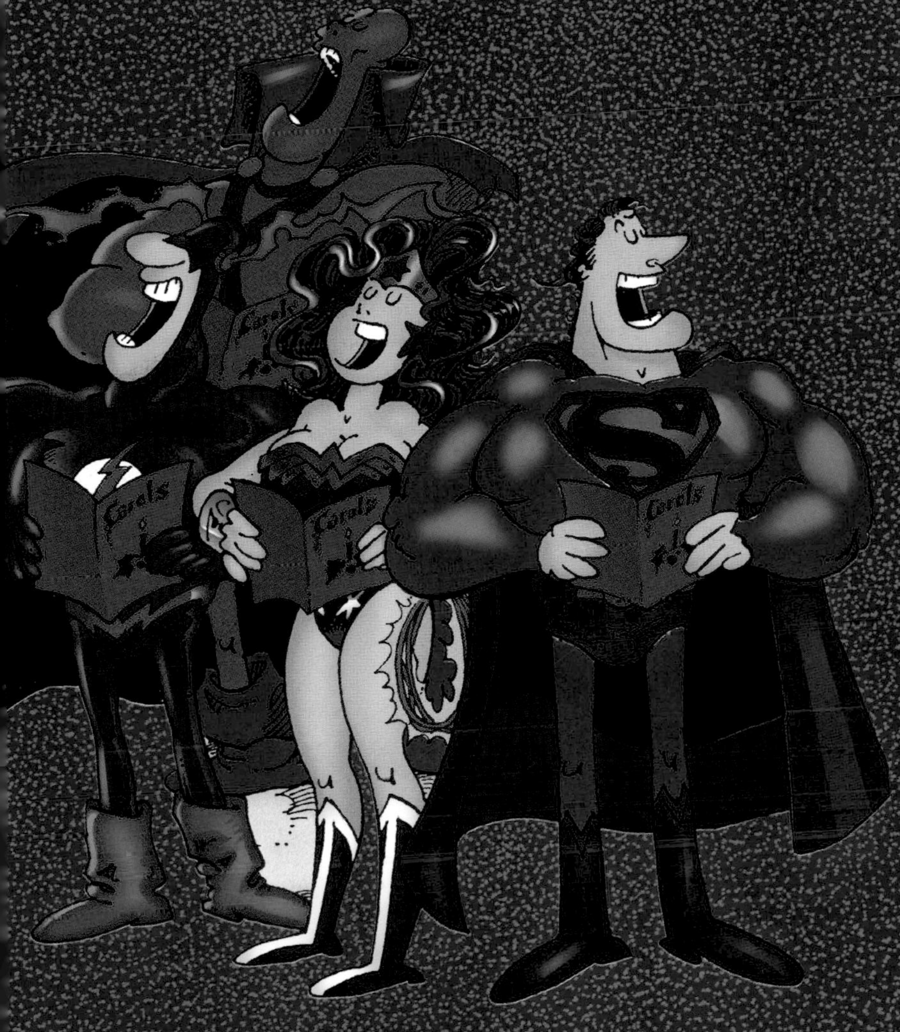
Carols
Carols
Carols
Carols

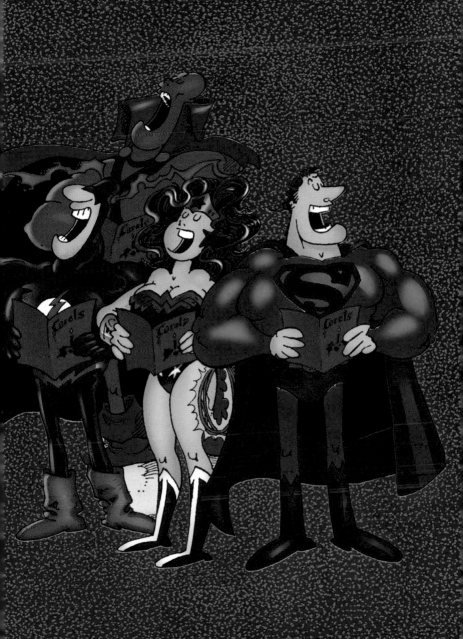

WHAT TEEN IS THIS?

"What Child Is This?"

What teen is this
In mask and cape
Who outwits villains so fleetly
And swings from yonder fire escape
To tie up the criminals neatly

"Robin!" is the name they cry
As he rounds up ne'er-do-wells easily
"Robin!" he replies with pride
And leaves them for Gotham P.D.

It was that teen
Who came to stay
At Wayne Manor so stately
And celebrated this Christmas Day
By hanging a star on the tree

"Robin!" Was the name I cried
As he toppled over the Christmas tree
"Sorry!" my young ward replied
And picked pine needles out of his booties

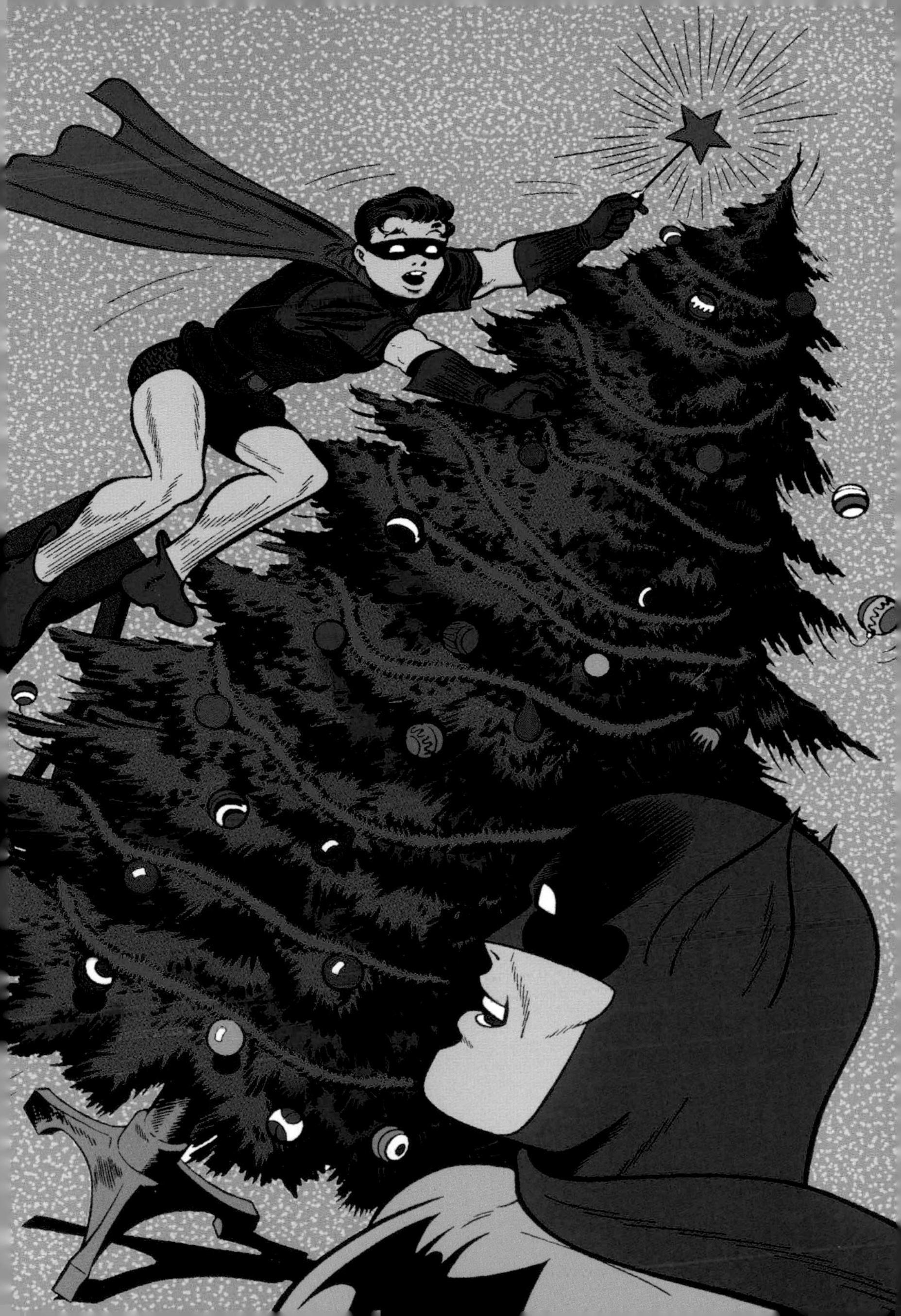

O LANTERN'S LIGHT

"Oh Holy Night"

O Lantern's light, the stars go on forever
Beyond the sector of two-eight-fourteen
O Lantern's light, the planets call together
For protection, from heroes in green
A blaze of light, an alien world rejoices
A brightest day, to banish blackest night

Hold up your rings, o see the Corps approaches
O evil outshined! O light to fight the dark
Green Lantern's light!
O light, Green Lantern's light!

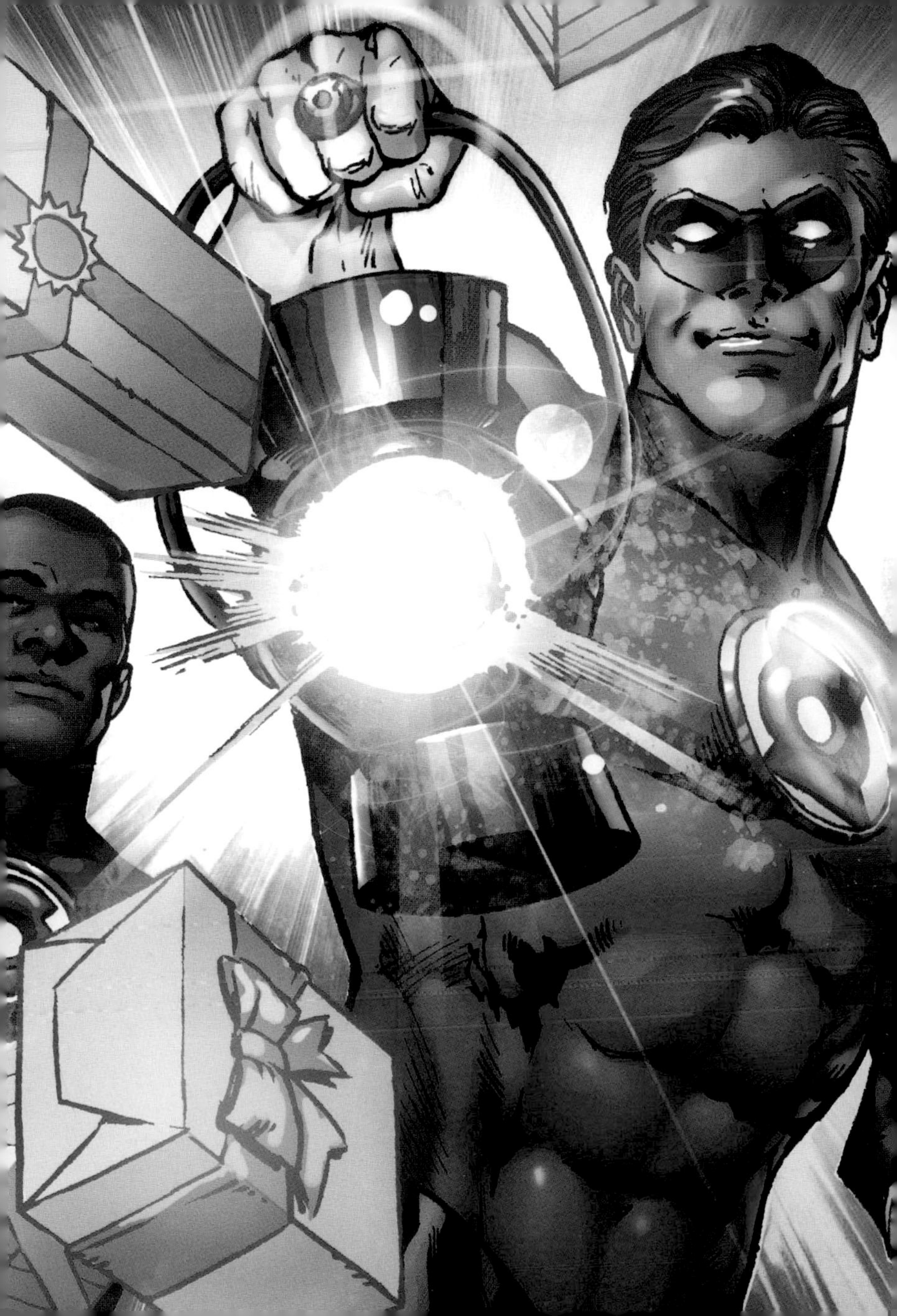

I SAW LOIS
KISSING SUPERMAN

"I Saw Mommy Kissing Santa Claus"

I saw Lois kissing Superman
Underneath the Daily Planet sign
They didn't see me climb
To the roof to wave goodbye
They thought that I was downstairs
Far away from prying eyes

I saw Lois kissing Superman
Right before he turned and flew away
Oh what trouble it would've been
If her boyfriend Clark had seen
Lois kissing Superman that day!

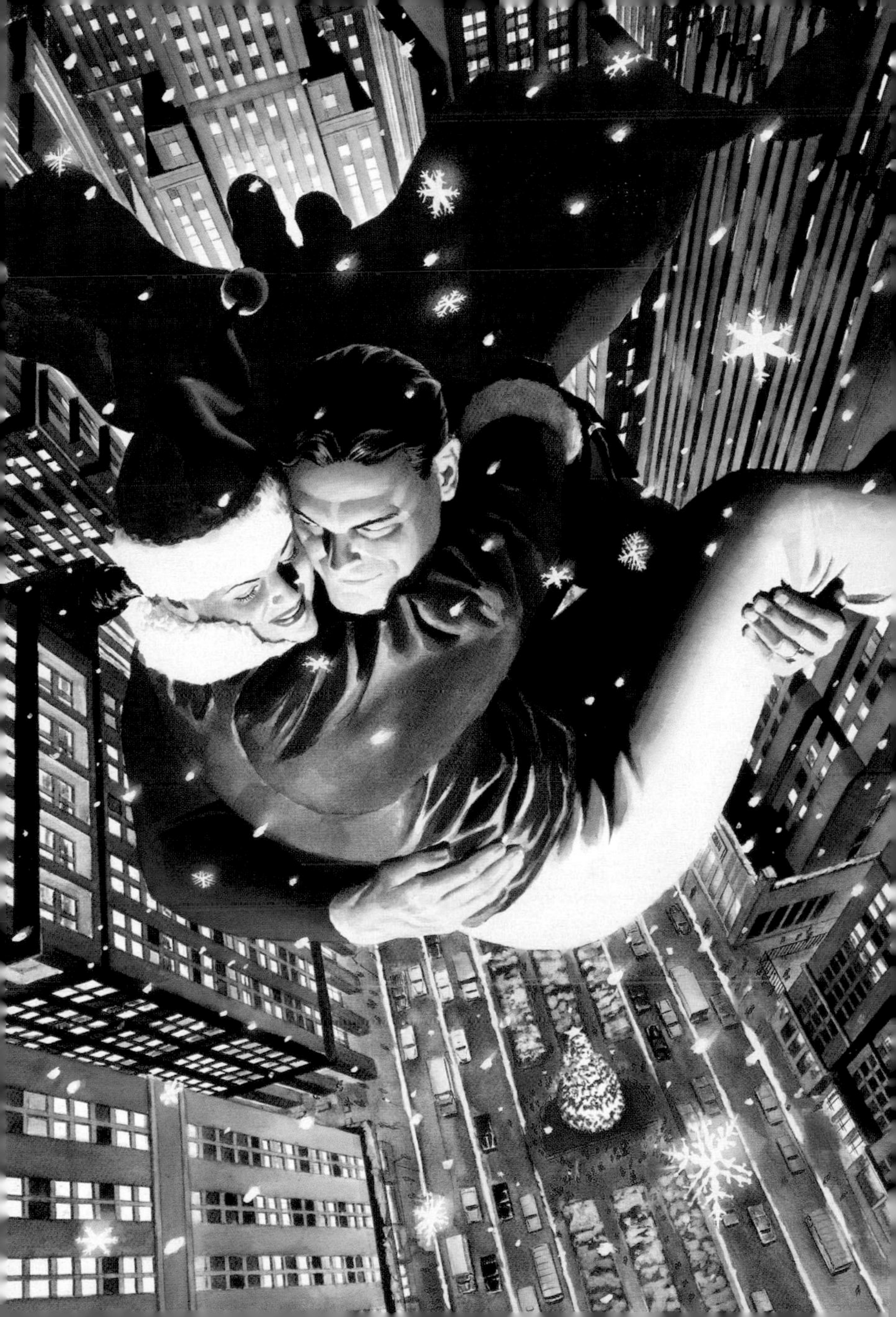

THE TWELVE DAYS OF VILLAINS

"The Twelve Days of Christmas"

On the first day of Christmas, from Arkham did they flee
With a kiss from Poison Ivy

On the second day of Christmas, from Arkham did they flee
Two Harvey Dents
With a kiss from Poison Ivy

On the third day of Christmas, from Arkham did they flee
Three Man-Bats
Two Harvey Dents
With a kiss from Poison Ivy

On the fourth day of Christmas, from Arkham did they flee
Four Killer Moths
Three Man-Bats
Two Harvey Dents
With a kiss from Poison Ivy

On the fifth day of Christmas, from Arkham did they flee
Five KGBeasts
Four Killer Moths
Three Man-Bats
Two Harvey Dents
With a kiss from Poison Ivy

On the sixth day of Christmas, from Arkham did they flee
Six Penguins clucking
Five KGBeasts
Four Killer Moths
Three Man-Bats
Two Harvey Dents
With a kiss from Poison Ivy

On the seventh day of Christmas, from Arkham did they flee
Seven Crows a'scaring
Six Penguins clucking
Five KGBeasts
Four Killer Moths
Three Man-Bats
Two Harvey Dents
With a kiss from Poison Ivy

On the eighth day of Christmas, from Arkham did they flee
Eight Faces Claying
Seven Crows a'scaring
Six Penguins clucking
Five KGBeasts
Four Killer Moths
Three Man-Bats
Two Harvey Dents
With a kiss from Poison Ivy

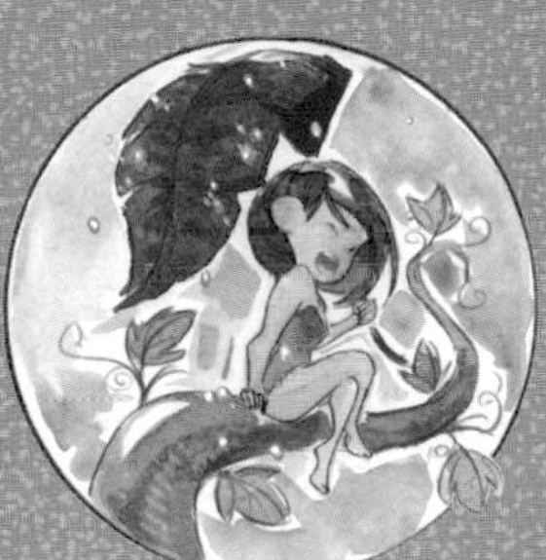

On the ninth day of Christmas, from Arkham did they flee
Nine Hatters hatting
Eight Faces Claying
Seven Crows a'scaring
Six Penguins clucking
Five KGBeasts
Four Killer Moths
Three Man-Bats
Two Harvey Dents
With a kiss from Poison Ivy

On the tenth day of Christmas, from Arkham did they flee
Ten Riddlers riddling
Nine Hatters hatting
Eight Faces Claying
Seven Crows a'scaring
Six Penguins clucking
Five KGBeasts
Four Killer Moths
Three Man-Bats
Two Harvey Dents
With a kiss from Poison Ivy

On the eleventh day of Christmas, from Arkham did they flee
Eleven Harleys Quinning
Ten Riddlers riddling
Nine Hatters hatting
Eight Faces Claying
Seven Crows a'scaring
Six Penguins clucking
Five KGBeasts
Four Killer Moths
Three Man-Bats
Two Harvey Dents
With a kiss from Poison Ivy

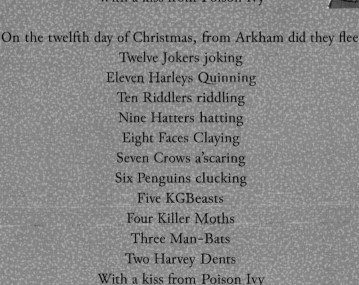

On the twelfth day of Christmas, from Arkham did they flee
Twelve Jokers joking
Eleven Harleys Quinning
Ten Riddlers riddling
Nine Hatters hatting
Eight Faces Claying
Seven Crows a'scaring
Six Penguins clucking
Five KGBeasts
Four Killer Moths
Three Man-Bats
Two Harvey Dents
With a kiss from Poison Ivy

UP ON THE ROOFTOP

"Up on the Rooftop"

Up on the rooftop lions paws
Out jumps Vixen with her claws
Down to the alley where bad guys wait
Animal powers have sealed their fate

Oh oh oh, you should've known
Oh oh oh, you should've known

Down from the rooftops,
SLASH, PUNCH, KICK!
Vixen's amulet has done the trick.

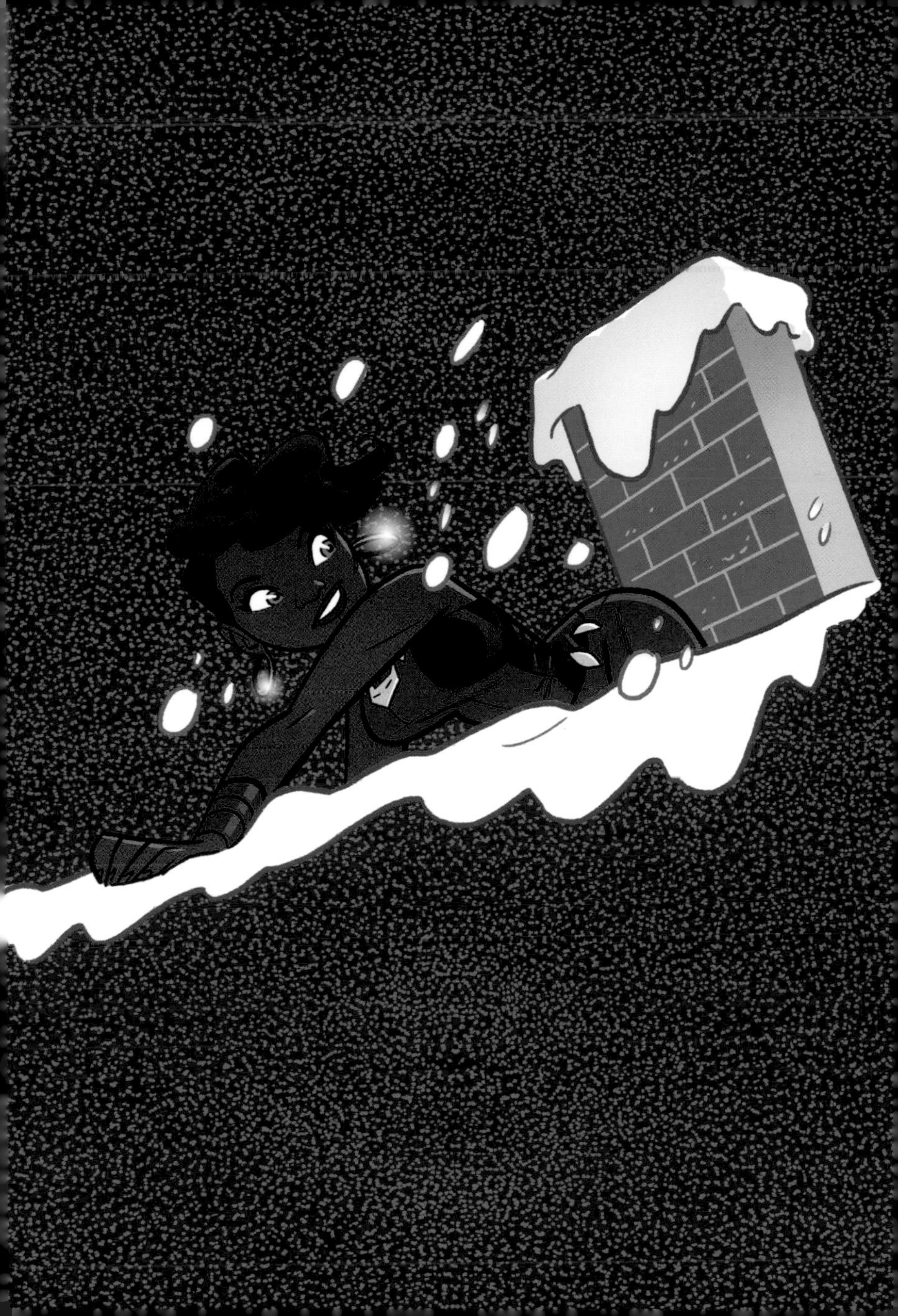

JINGLE BELLS, HARLEY'S SWELL

"Jingle Bells"

Jingle Bells
Harley's swell!
Batman's just okay
My new look is off the hook
So who needs Mr. J?

Dashing through the streets
From a speeding Batmobile
Nearly Christmas Eve
So much more to steal!
(HA HA HA!)
Mallet in my hand
Making smiles bright
What fun it is to smash and grab
On a frosty winter's night!

OHHHH
Jingle Bells
Arkham cells
Watch me get away
Harley Quinn is gonna win
On a Merry Christmas Day!

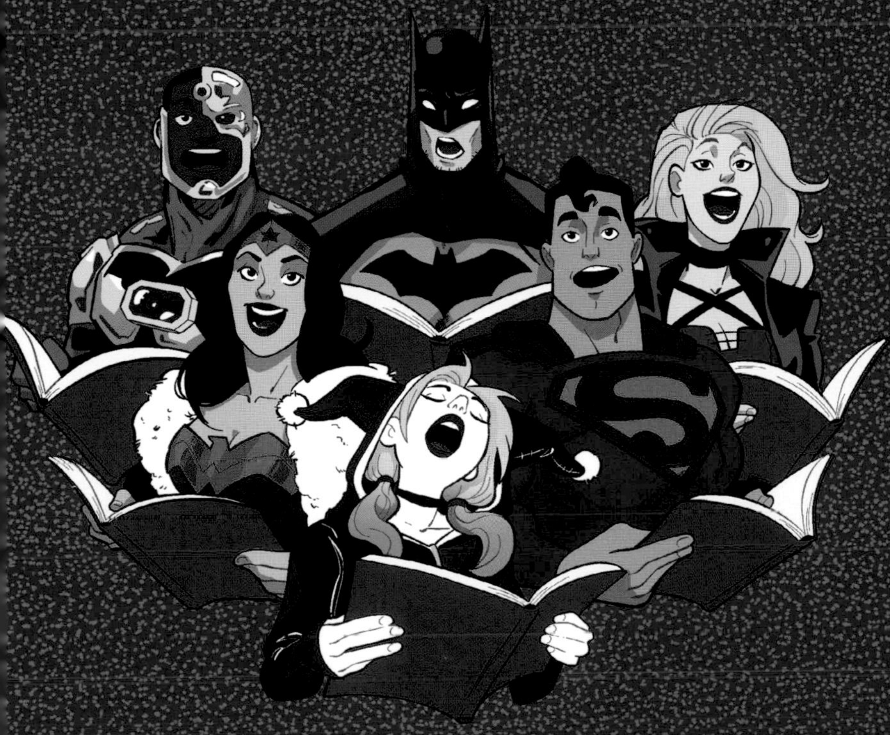

I'M SCREAMING FOR A FRIGHT CHRISTMAS

"I'm Dreaming of a White Christmas"

I'm screaming for a fright Christmas
Just like the fear we used to know
Where the shadows beckoned and
children reckoned with things
Lurking down below

I'm screaming for a fright Christmas
For every helpless Gothamite
May their days be scary as night
And may all their Christmases be frights

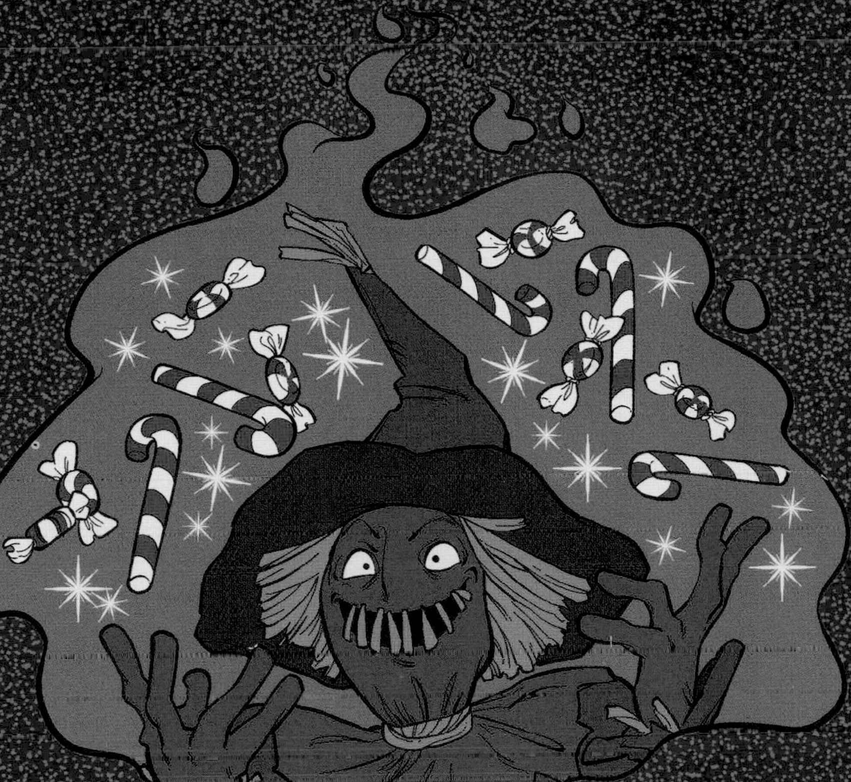

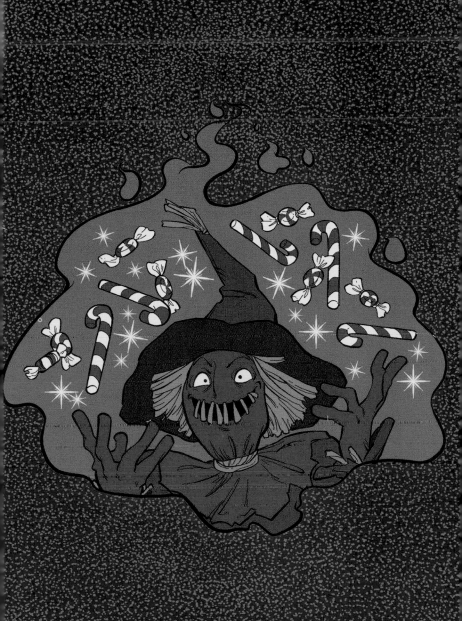

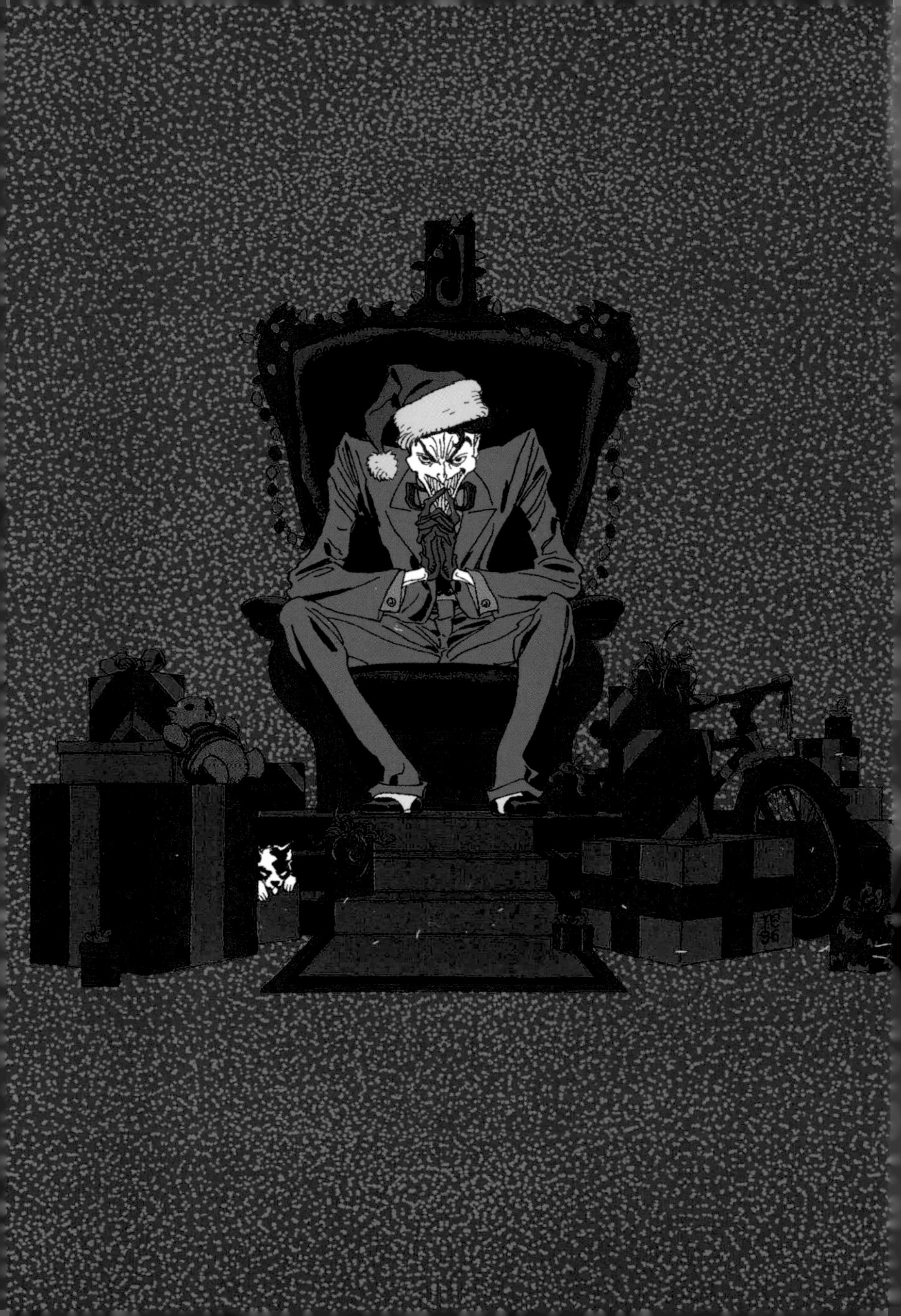

IT'S A JOKE!

"Let It Snow"

Oh my smile, to some, is frightful
But the crimes are so delightful
So although it might scare some folks
It's a joke, it's a joke, it's a joke!

Well my wind-up teeth are chattering
And the acid flower is splattering
Don't forget to tip your waitstaff
Have a laugh, have a laugh, have a laugh!

I developed a sense of style
When I fell in that chemical vat
Now I paint the whole town with smiles
And stay one step ahead of the Bat!

Other villains can never match me
And the Batman may always catch me
But as long as we have some laughs
It's a gas, it's a gas, it's a gas!

THERE GOES BIZARRO

"Here Comes Santa Claus"

THERE GOES BIZARRO
THERE GOES BIZARRO
RIGHT UP BIZARRO LANE

ME AM WEAK
AND ME CAN'T SPEAK
AND VULNERABLE TO PAIN!

ME AM HERO
SUPERMAN ZERO
ME NOT CHALKY AND WHITE
AND SUPERMAN BETTER NOT SAY HIS PRAYERS
'CUZ ME NOT HERE FOR A FIGHT!

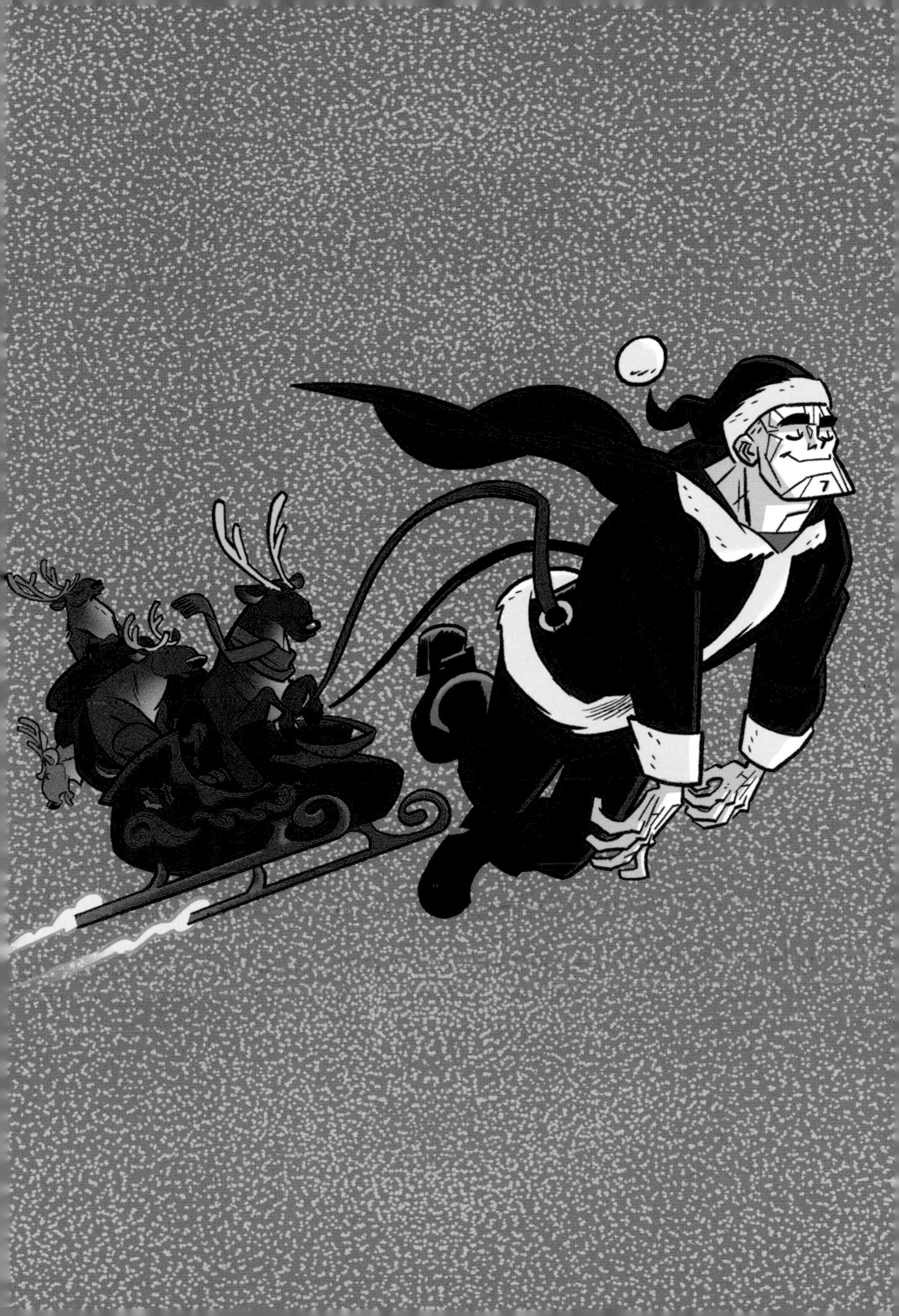

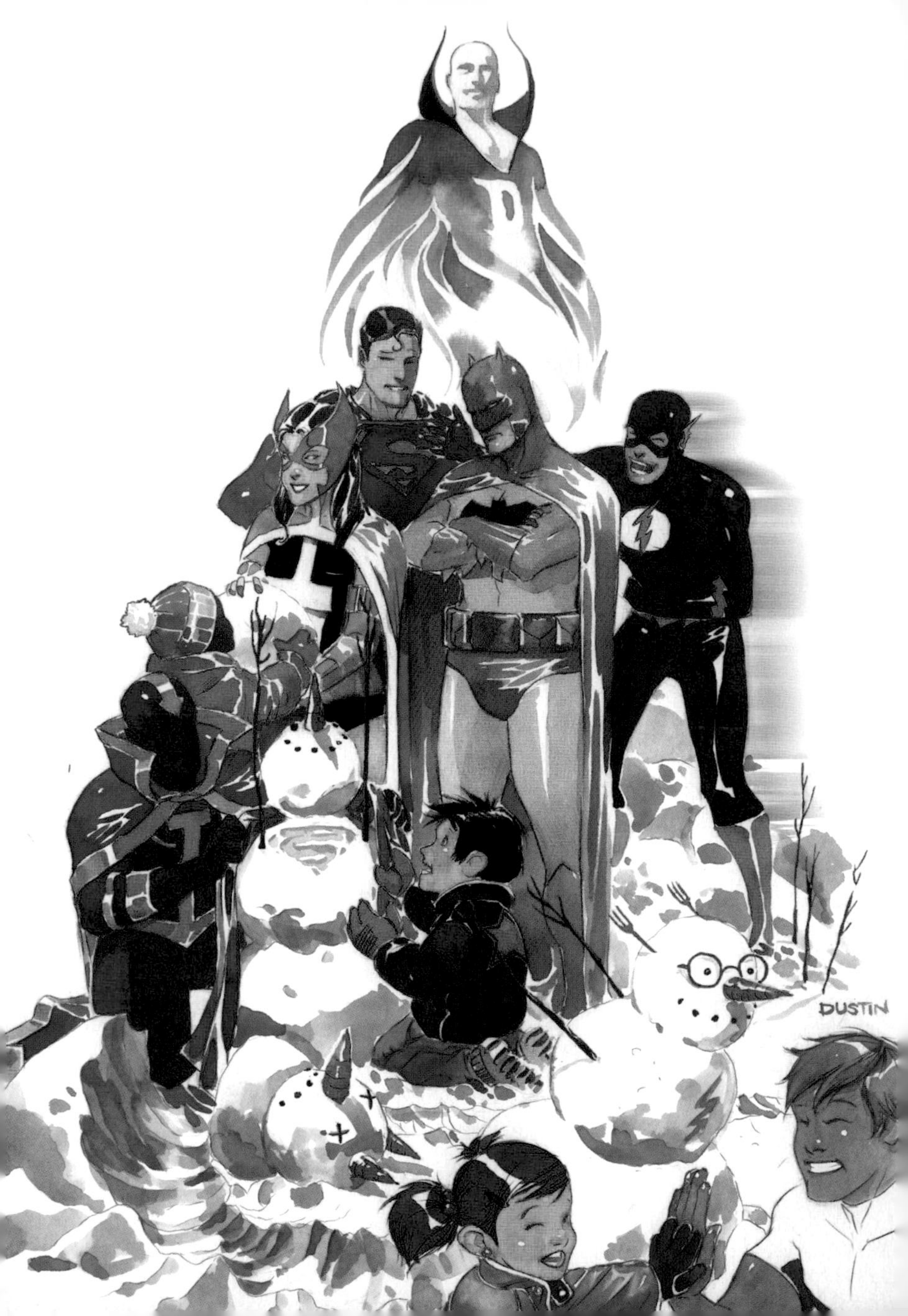
DUSTIN

THE DEADMAN SONG

"The Dreidel Song"

Deadman, Deadman, Deadman
An acrobat so brave
Deadman, Deadman, Deadman
Yourself you couldn't save

Well
I knew a great performer
His name was Boston Brand
But no one could've warned him
How rapidly he'd land

Oh
Deadman, Deadman, Deadman
Our bodies you possess
And when you've solved your mystery
You'll achieve eternal rest

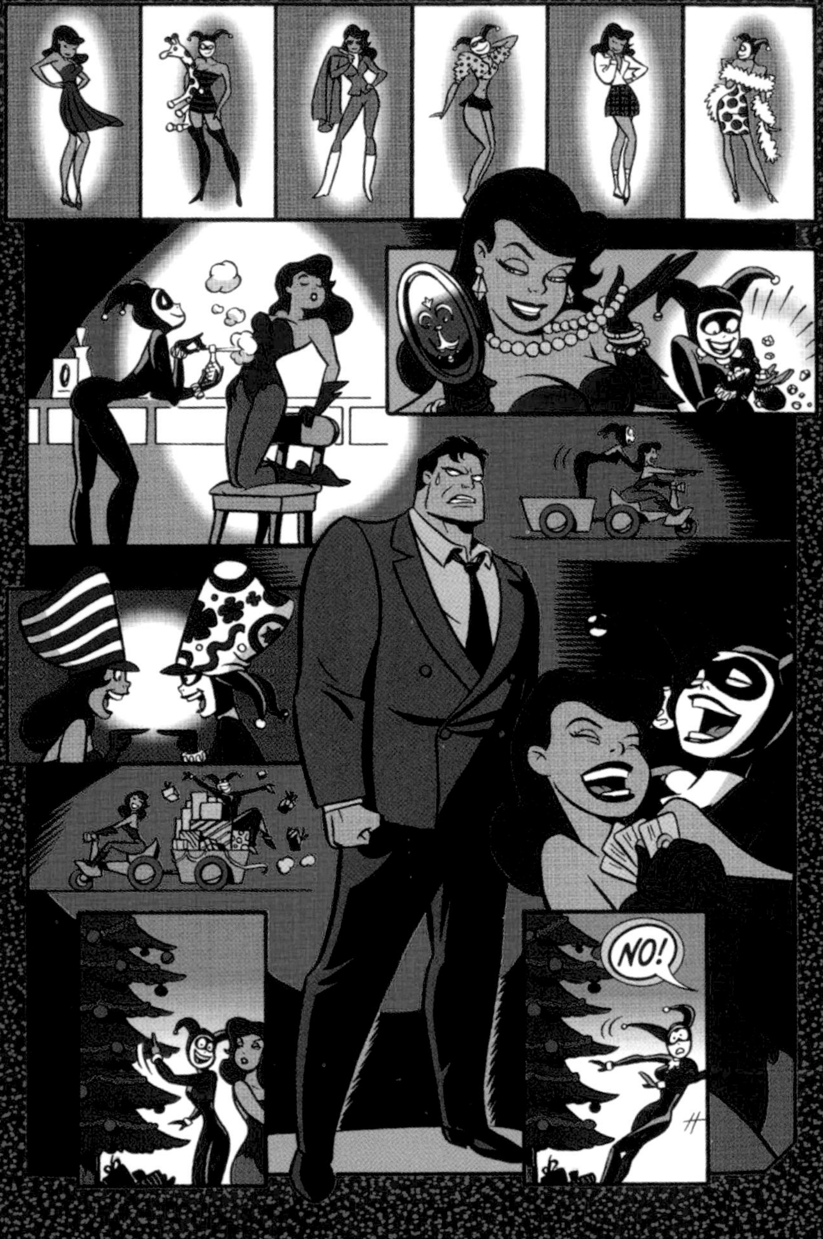
NO!

THE HARLEY AND THE IVY

"The Holly and the Ivy"

The Harley and the Ivy,
When they go hit the town,
Of every glamorous villainess,
Pam and Harley take the crown

O, the running up of tabs
And the trying on of clothes
And a gentle peck from Ivy's lips
Leaves the poor guards comatose

While Harley starts the engine
And Ivy plies her charms
They disappear with shopping bags
Without setting off alarms

O, the swiping of the jewelry
And the modeling the gowns
It's Christmastime for criminals
Be they botanists or clowns

BIRDY, IT'S COLD OUTSIDE

"Baby, It's Cold Outside"

You really can't stay
(But Birdy, it's cold outside)
I've got an early day
(But Birdy it's cold outside)
I think you'll be fine,
out in the snow
(I seem to have misplaced my bow)

It's obvious that you're stalling
(Can't you see I'm falling?)
Don't make me scream the whole
house apart
(Screaming "you can stay"
is a start)
Your cheesiness is appalling
(Do you hear
those lovebirds calling?)
Maybe you can sleep in the yard
(Shoot an arrow straight
through my heart)

It's been a long night
(But Birdy, I've lost my phone)
There's villains to fight
(Can't let you do that alone)
You've been a fun date
(It's not even really late)
But take the hint
(My beard oil smells
like peppermint . . .)
Pretty sure
you dropped this quiver
(Look at how your touch
makes me shiver)
You think you're such
a charming guy
(I know when I've hit the bullseye)

You really can't stay
(Too late, it's morning)
Birdy, it's cold outside.

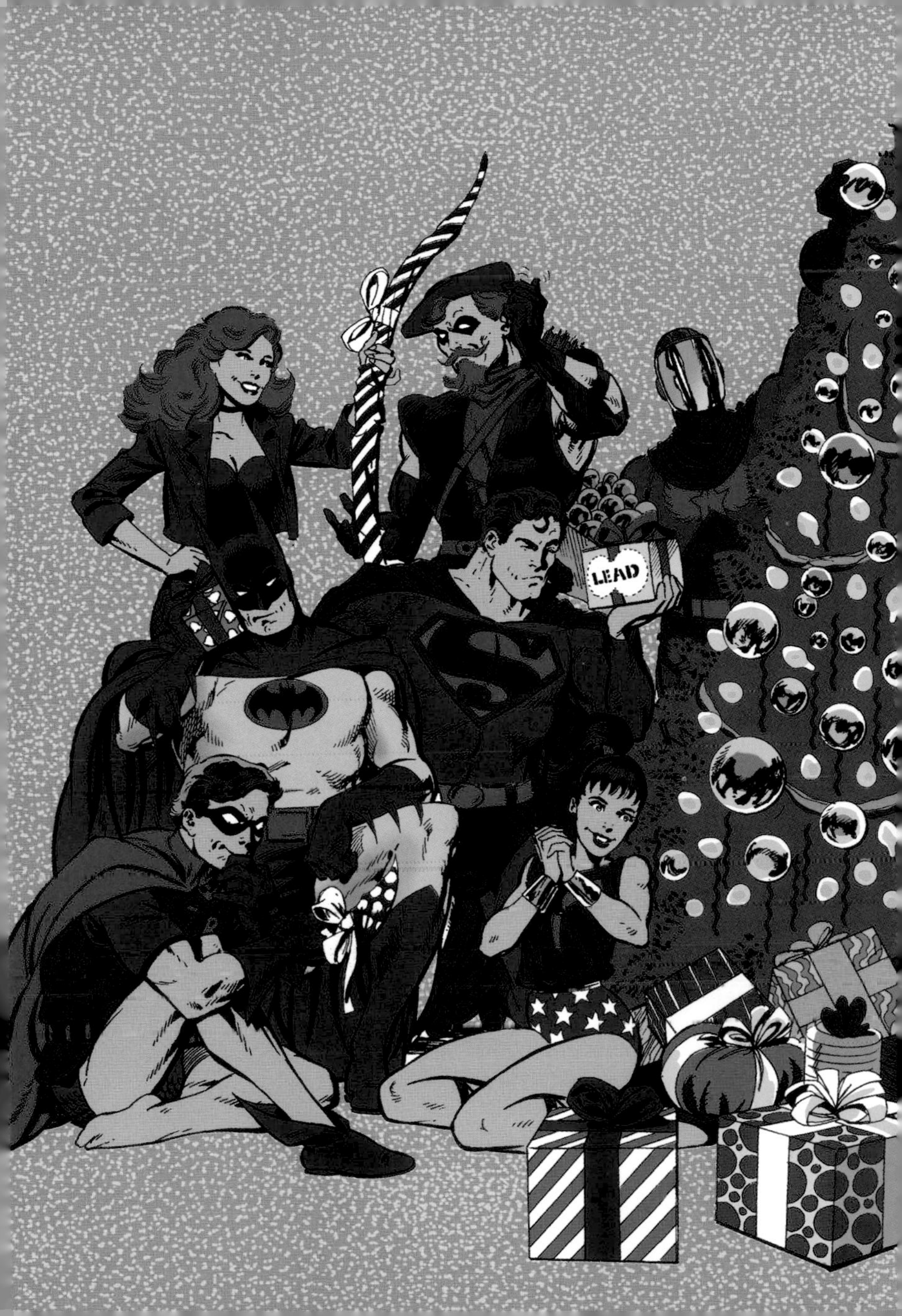
LEAD

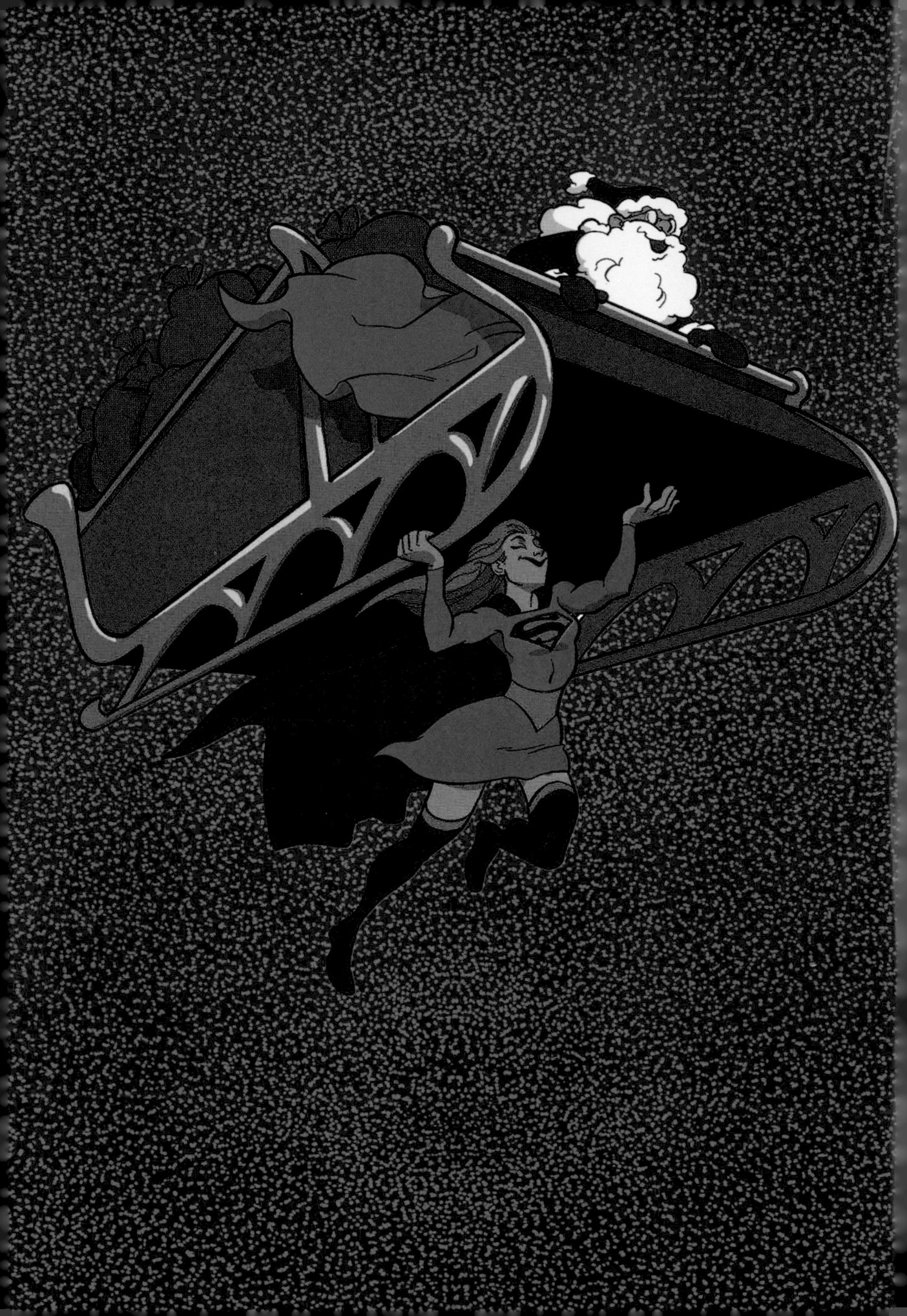

JOY TO THE GIRL

"Joy to the World"

Joy to the girl
From old Krypton
Let Earth receive her might!

Protecting all humanity
From villains and calamity
And setting wrong things right
And setting wrong things right
And setting the wrongest of the wrong things right!

DO YOU FEEL WHAT I FEEL?

"Do You Hear What I Hear?"

Said the Swamp Thing to the little leaf
Do you feel what I feel?
Way deep inside, little leaf
Do you feel what I feel?

A calm, a calm
Rippling through the Green
Whatever could it mean?
Whatever could it mean?

Said the little leaf to the Swamp Thing
Do you hear what I hear?
Said the little leaf to the Swamp Thing
Do you hear what I hear?

A wind, a wind
Blowing through the trees
Bringing peace and joy to the Green
Bringing peace and joy to the Green

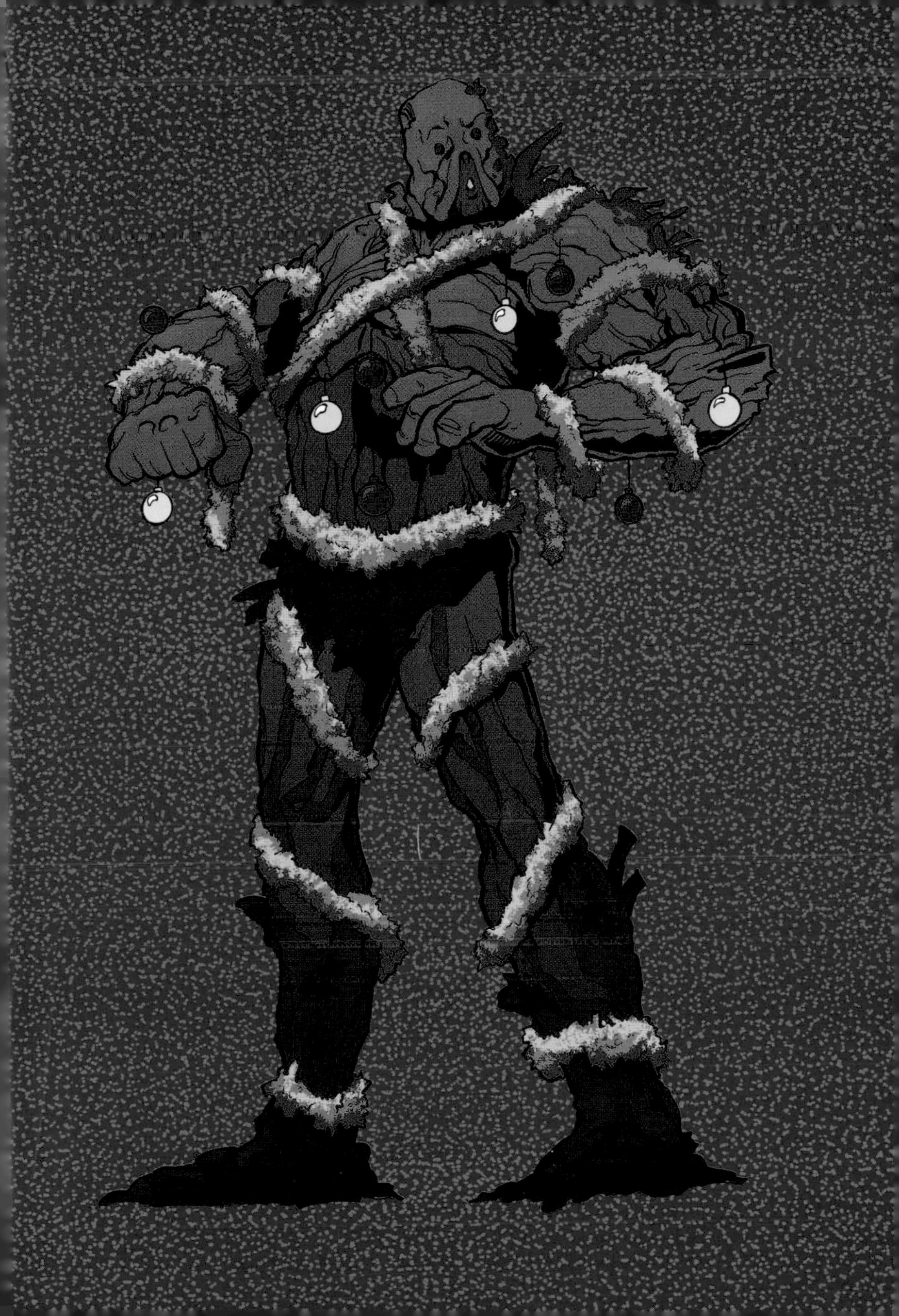

WE TWO QUEENS
OF THEMYSCIRA

"We Three Kings of Orient Are"

We two queens of Themyscira
Diana and Hippolyta
Island hidden, men forbidden
Or face the wrath of Hera

O, isle of wonder, isle of light
Learn compassion, learn to fight
Far from man, they train and plan
To battle for what is right

Far from all humanity's strife
Hippolyta birthed a new life
Shaped from clay, she found a way
To fight for the world outside

O, isle of fearsome Amazons
Soldiers evil can't outrun
May not trust us, but for justice
All will raise their swords as one

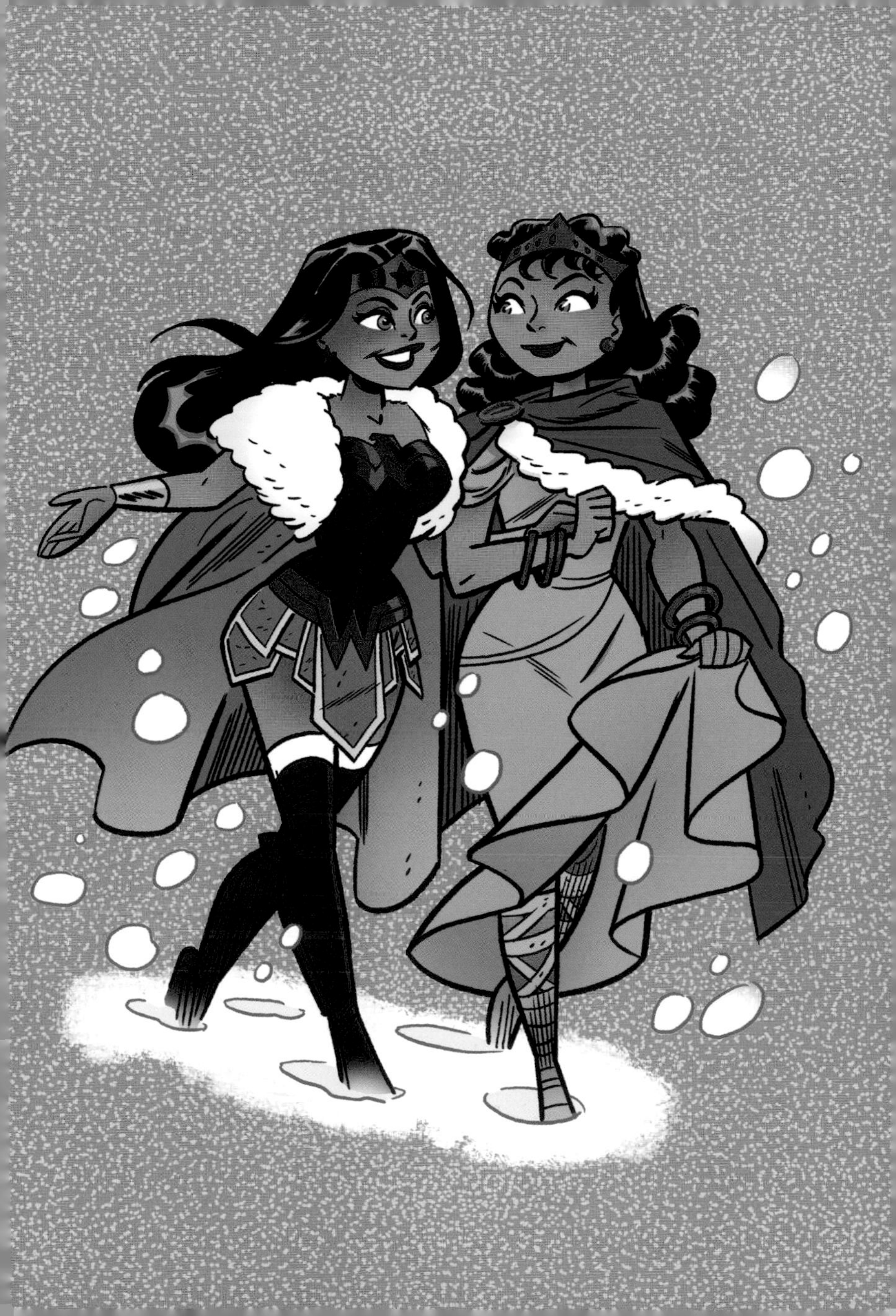

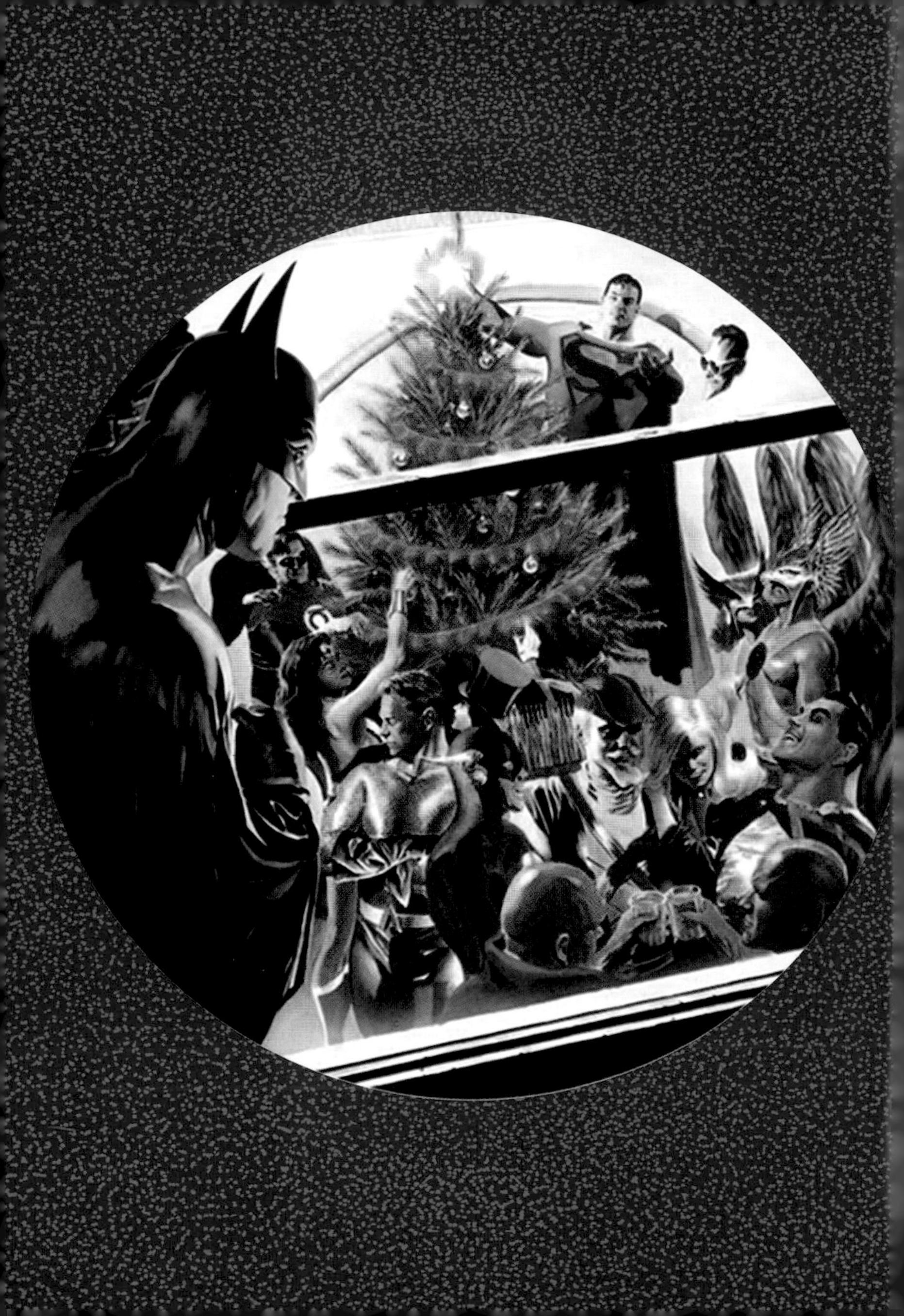

I SAW TWO HAWKS

"I Saw Two Ships"

I saw two hawks come swooping in
From Thanagar, from Thanagar
I saw two hawks come swooping in
To battle for Midway City

The hawks flew in from the depths of space
From Thanagar, from Thanagar
Armed with Nth Metal sword and mace
To fight for our Midway City

I heard their cry as they faced their foes,
"For Thanagar! For Thanagar!"
And struck them down with colossal blows
And rescued all Midway City!

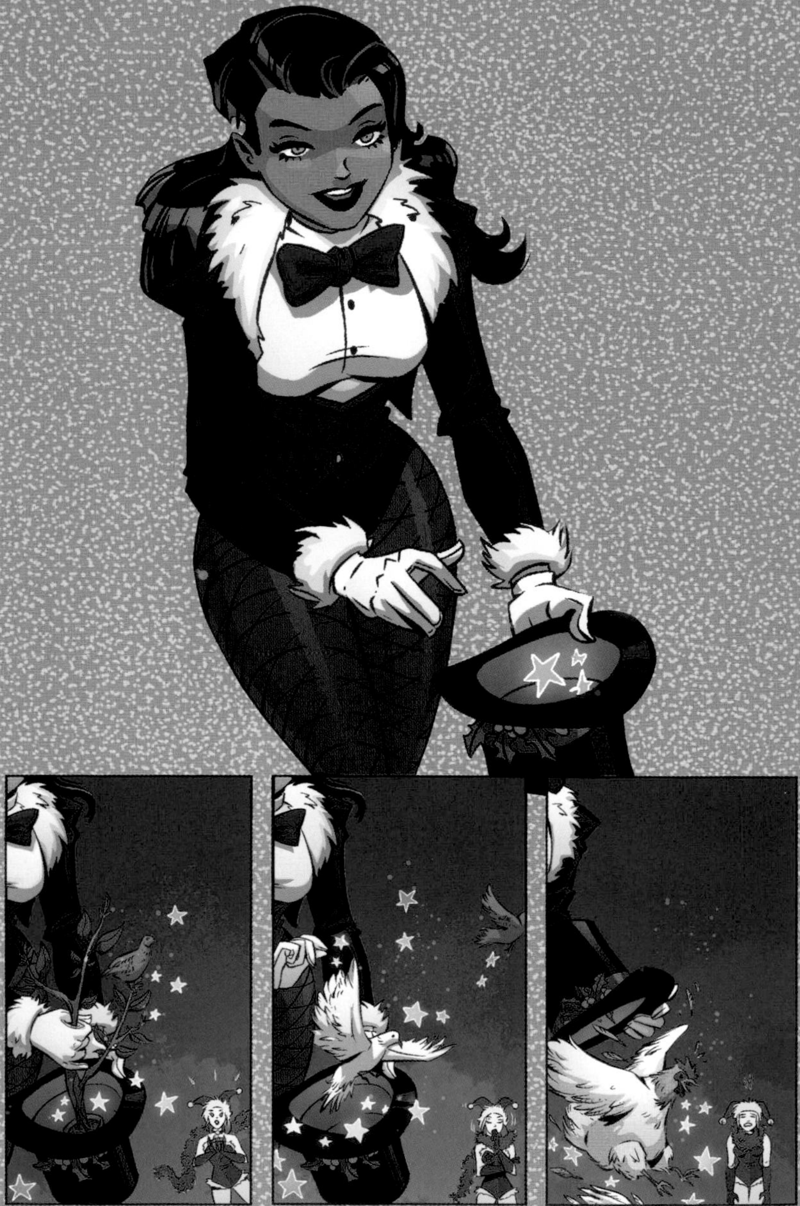

SHE MADE A
RABBIT DISAPPEAR

"It Came Upon a Midnight Clear"

She made a rabbit disappear
She vanished it into a hat
She said some words that weren't quite clear
And that was the end of that

She'll do the same to villains too
If they and Zatanna cross paths
She'll charm you with some backwards speech
And you'll disappear in a flash

Ehs edam a tibbar raeppasid
Ehs dehsinav ti otni a tah
Ehs dias emos sdrow taht t'nerew etiuq raelc
Dna taht saw eht dne fo taht

TRY BEST YE MERRY METAL MEN

"God Rest Ye Merry, Gentlemen"

Try best ye merry Metal Men
Keep villainy at bay
Remember Doctor Magnus
Constructed you that way
To save the world from evil-doers
Whose paths had gone astray
Out of Tin, Platinum, Iron, Lead, and Gold
Iron and Gold
Out of Mercury and Iron and Gold

Contort yourselves to any shape
Your circuitry allows
Your enemies will not escape
There's no stopping you now!
As nets and springs and shiny things
You'll save the day and how
Out of Tin, Platinum, Iron, Lead, and Gold
Iron and Gold
Out of Mercury and Iron and Gold

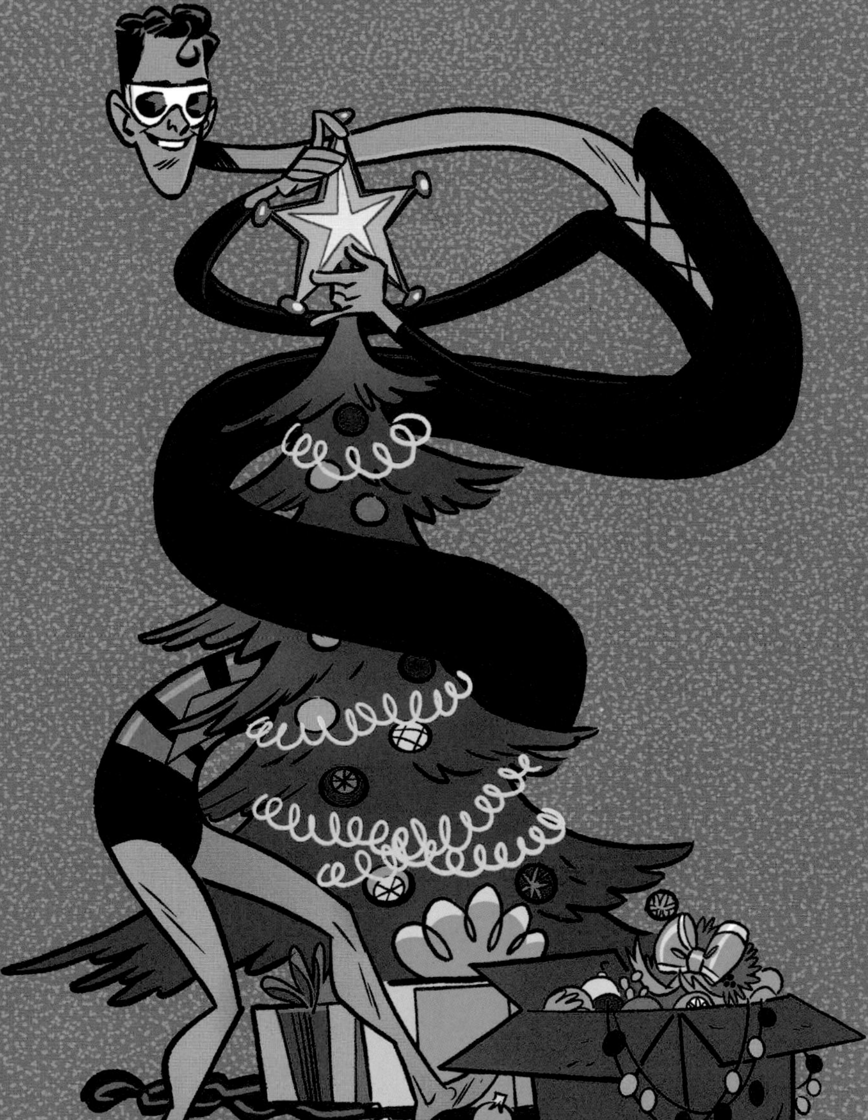

LITTLE RUBBER BOY

"Little Drummer Boy"

"Stop," they told me
A rubber-dub-dub
"You're so annoying,"
A rubber-dub-dub
"We hate the sound it makes"
A rubber-dub-dub
"Each time you change your shape!"
A rubber-dub-dub, rubber-dub-dub, rubber-dub-bub

But I'm a Plastic Man,
A rubber-dub-dub
I have to stretch and span!
A rubber-dub-dub
To bend and never break
A rubber-dub-dub
There's no shape I can't take!
A rubber-dub-dub, rubber-dub-dub, rubber-dub-bub

But it bothers them
A rubber-dub-dub
Join the club!

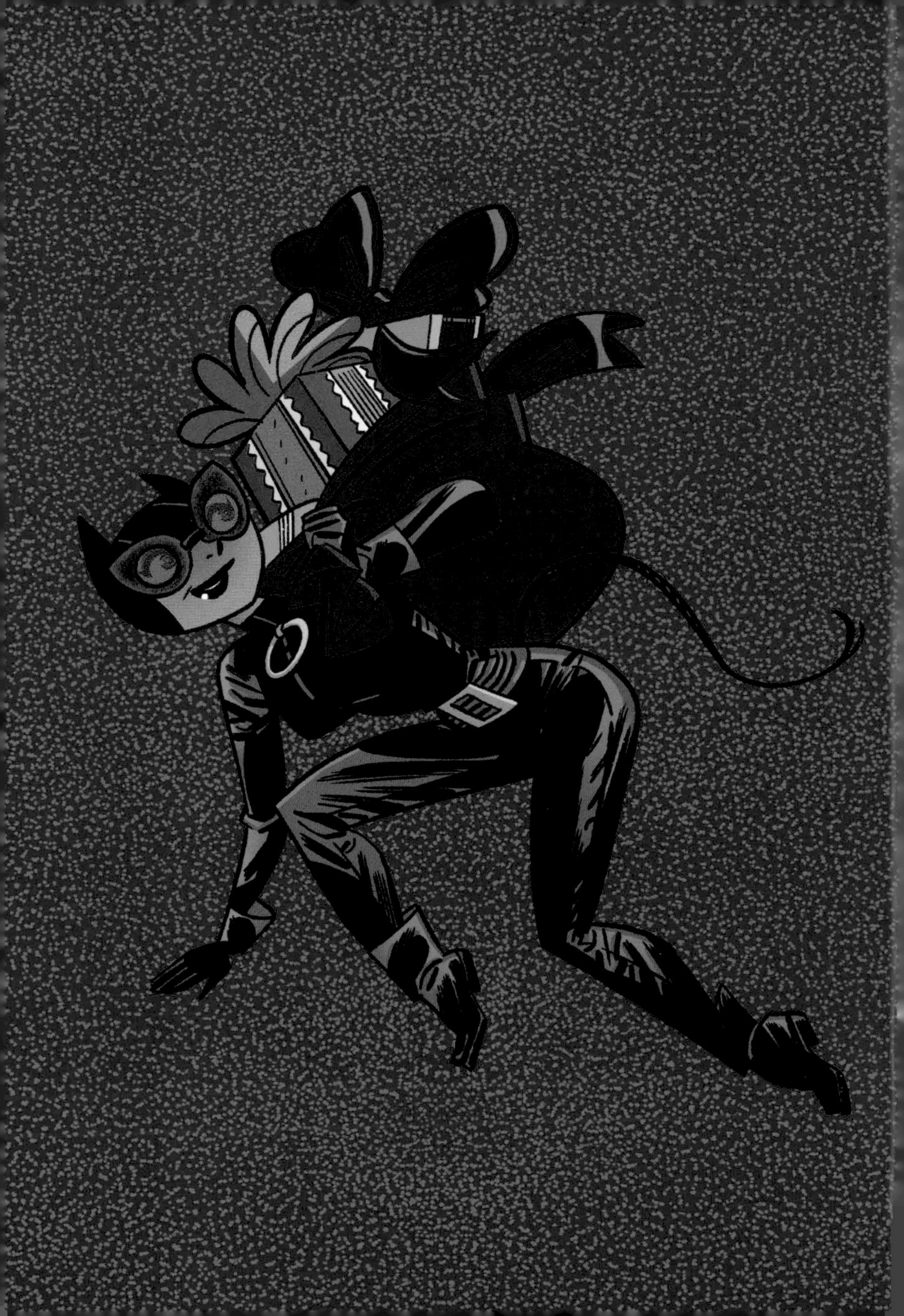

BATMAN BABY

"Santa Baby"

Batman baby, just let me get away this one time—It's fine
I won't do it again
Batman baby, you don't have to be such a Dark Knight

Batman baby, and why not let me keep the jewels too—
Won't you?
They'll look better on me
Batman baby, just let me have a warning this time

Think of all the fun we'd have
If you didn't think that crime was quite so bad
Imagine all the joy it'd bring
If you let me get away with everything

Batman baby, I love to watch you BIFF! BAM! and POW—
Meow
You put on quite a show
Batman baby, so be a dear and just let me go

Batman baby, just one more thing and then I must dash—
the cash
Let me take it with me
Batman baby, we'll split it fity-fifty—alright?

HAVE YOURSELF A VERY LITTLE CHRISTMAS

"Have Yourself a Merry Little Christmas"

Have yourself a very little Christmas
Tiny as can be
From now on your problems are too small to see

Have yourself a very little Christmas
Barely Atom-sized
From now on your troubles with be miniaturized

Come with me and we'll all traverse
Through the Microverse this year
Disappear to the human eye
And bring nuclei good cheer

At this scale, a Christmas lasts forever
Time and space allow
Hang a White Dwarf Star and I will show you how
To have yourself a very little Christmas now

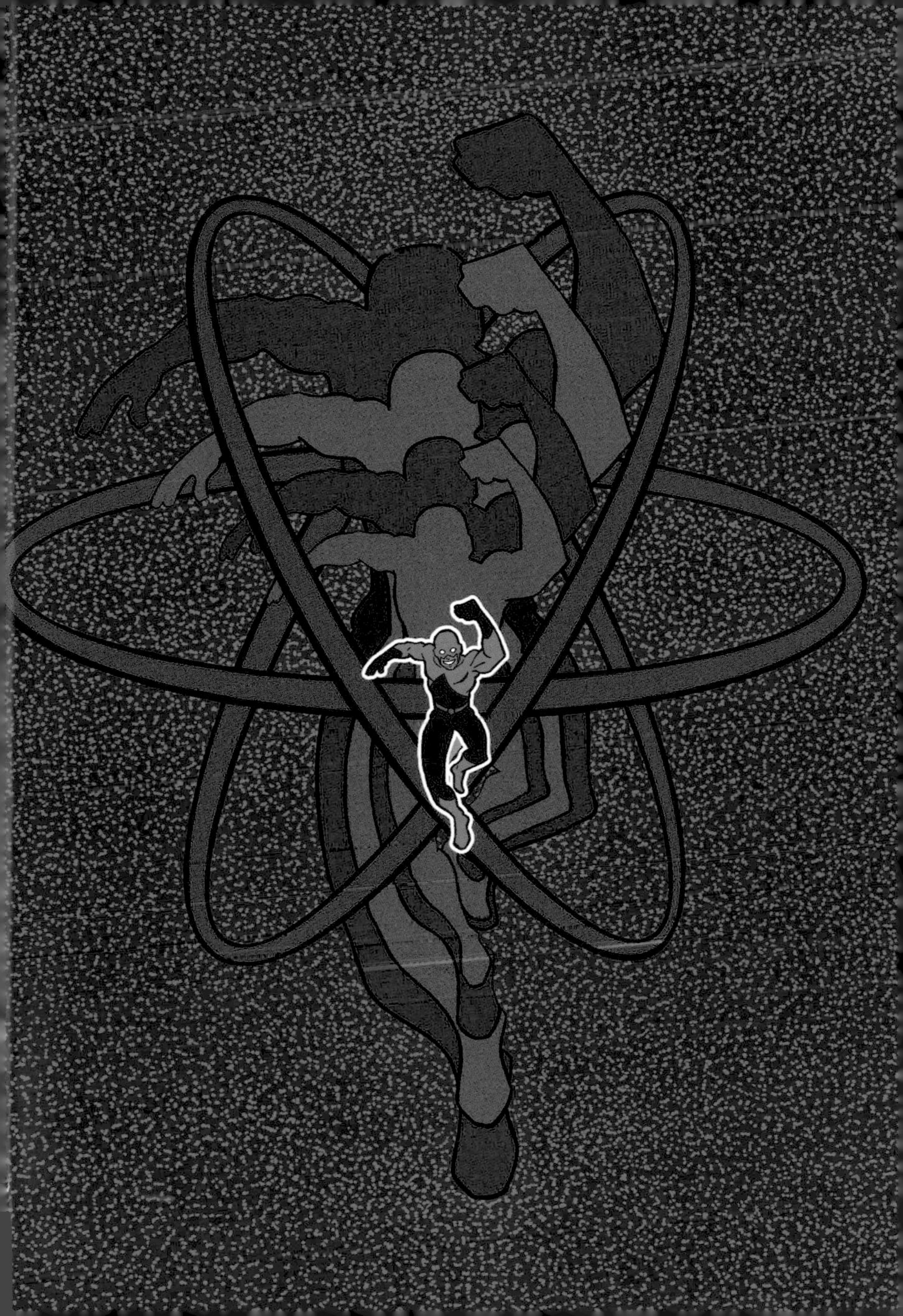

DECK THE HALLS (WITH YOUR PAL HARLEY)

"Deck the Halls (with Boughs of Holly)"

Deck the halls with your pal Harley
Ha-ha-ha-ha-ha, ha-ha-ha-ha
Try to stop me, you'll be sorry
Ha-ha-ha-ha-ha, ha-ha-ha-ha

If you say I didn't nail it
Ha-ha-ha, ha-ha-ha, ha-ha-ha
Get a face full of my mallet
Ha-ha-ha-ha-ha, ha-ha-ha-ha

Shower me with jewels and money
Ha-ha-ha-ha-ha, ha-ha-ha-ha
Or things will get a lot less funny
Ha-ha-ha-ha-ha, ha-ha-ha-ha

Stupid Bats will never find me
Ha-ha-ha, ha-ha-ha, ha-ha-ha
What do you mean "he's right behind me?"
Ha-ha ha-ha ha, ha-ha—oh no!

Oh well! Happy Harley-days!

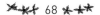 68

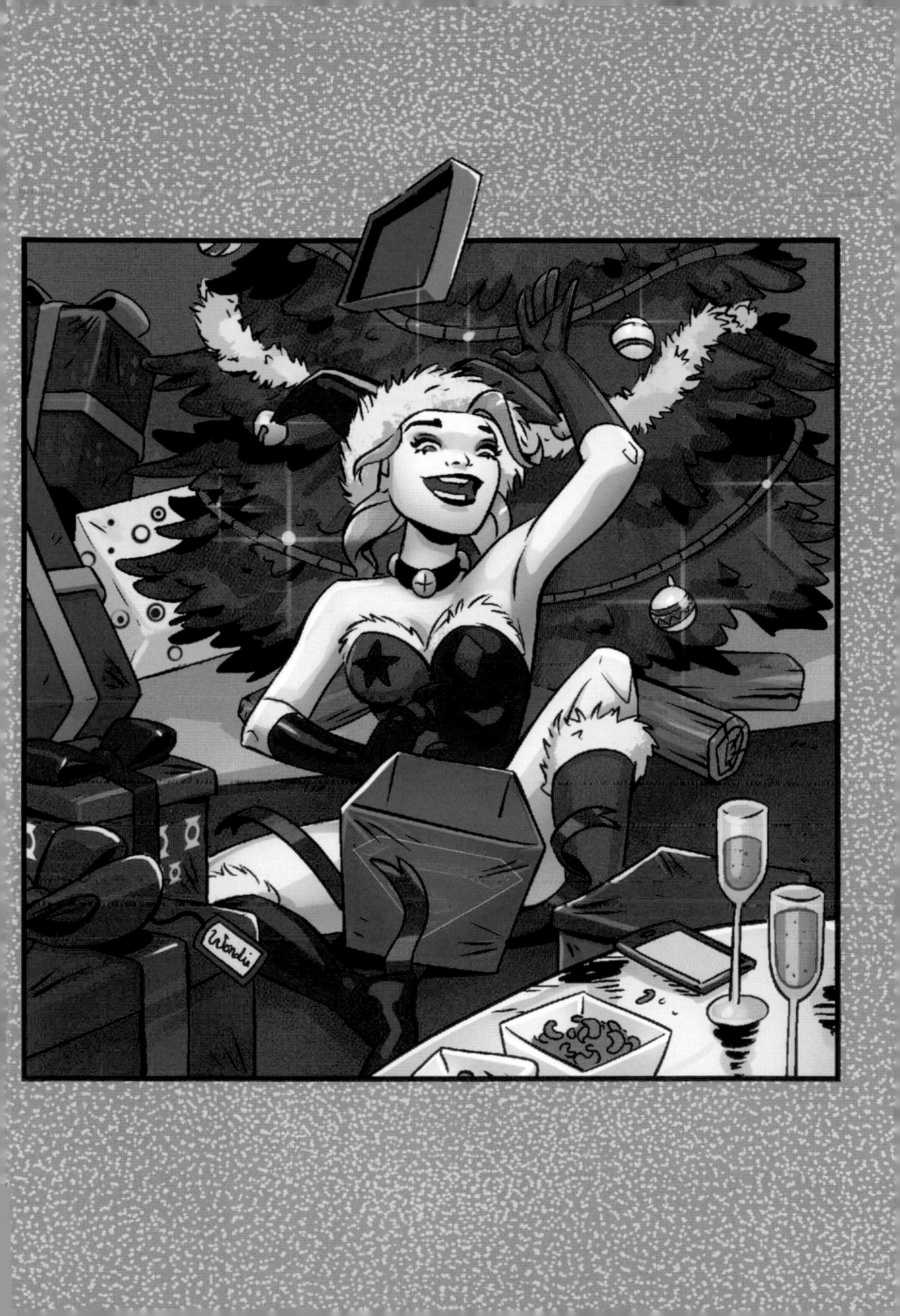
Wondie

ART CREDITS

7: Ro Stein (pencils), Ted Brandt (inks), 2020

9: *Batman* (Vol. 1) #27, 1945, Jack Burnley

10: *Action Comics* (Vol. 1) #1005, 2016, Francis Manapul

12: *Sensation Comics* (Vol. 1) #38, 1942, Harry G. Peter

15: *The Flash* (Vol. 4) #13, 2016, Dave Johnson

16: *Teen Titans Go!* (Vol. 1) #25, 2005, Sean Galloway

19: *DC Universe Holiday Special* #1, "Somewhere Beyond the Sea," 2008, Ian Churchill
(pencils, inks), Bob Rivard (colors)

20: J. Bone, 2020

23: *DCU Holiday Bash III* #1, 1998, Sergio Aragonés

25: *Batman* (Vol. 1) #33, 1946, Dick Sprang

27: *Green Lantern: Larfleeze Christmas Special* #1, 2010, Ivan Reis

29: *Mythology: The DC Comics Art of Alex Ross*, 2003, Alex Ross

30: *Batman Li'l Gotham* (Vol. 1), 2014, Dustin Nguyen

31: *Batman Li'l Gotham* (Vol. 1), 2014, Dustin Nguyen

32: *Batman Li'l Gotham* (Vol. 2), 2014, Dustin Nguyen

33: *Batman Li'l Gotham* (Vol. 2), 2014, Dustin Nguyen

35: J. Bone, 2020

37: Ro Stein (pencils), Ted Brandt (inks)

39: Ro Stein (pencils), Ted Brandt (inks)

40: *Batman: The Long Halloween* #3, 1996, Tim Sale (pencils, inks), Gregory Wright (colors)

43: J. Bone, 2020

44: *DC Holiday Special '09* #1, 2009, Dustin Nguyen

46: *The Batman Adventures Holiday Special* #1, 1994, Ronnie Del Carmen

49: *Christmas with the Super-Heroes* #1, 1988, John Byrne

50: Ro Stein (pencils), Ted Brandt (inks)

53: Ro Stein (pencils), Ted Brandt (inks)

55: J. Bone, 2020

56: *Mythology: The DC Comics Art of Alex Ross*, 2003, Alex Ross

58: *DC Rebirth Holiday Special* #1, 2016, Elsa Charretier (pencils, inks), Hi-Fi Design (colors)

61: J. Bone, 2020

62: J. Bone, 2020

64: J. Bone, 2020

67: Ro Stein (pencils), Ted Brandt (inks)

69: *DC Rebirth Holiday Special* #1, 2016, Elsa Charretier (pencils, inks), Hi-Fi Design (colors)

Acknowledgments

For my nephew, Jack Parker, who right now can say only "Carly Quinn."

About the Author

DANIEL KIBBLESMITH is an Emmy-nominated TV writer for places like Netflix and *The Late Show with Stephen Colbert*. He has written comics for DC and Marvel, comedy for *The New Yorker* and *McSweeney's*, and was a founding editor of ClickHole. He is married to his favorite author, Jennifer Wright.

Special Contributing Artists

J. BONE is an Eisner Award-nominated Canadian comic book artist and writer. His credits include *Batman: The Brave and the Bold* and *Super Friends* for DC Comics, *Rocketeer: Hollywood Horror* and *Rocketeer at War* for IDW, and *The Saviors* for Image Comics. He was the inker on the Eisner Award-winning one-shot *Batman/The Spirit* as well as *The Spirit* ongoing series with artist Darwyn Cooke.

RO STEIN AND TED BRANDT are a comics producing partnership working out of the UK. They are best known for their work on *Crowded* for Image Comics, which has been nominated for multiple awards.

Copyright 2020 © DC Comics.
All DC characters and elements © & ™ DC Comics.
WB SHIELD: ™ & © Warner Bros. Entertainment, Inc. (f20)

Library of Congress Cataloging-in-Publication Data available.

ISBN 978-1-7972-0795-7

Manufactured in China.

MIX
Paper from
responsible sources
FSC
www.fsc.org   FSC™ C104723

Design by Jon Glick.

10 9 8 7 6 5 4 3 2 1

Chronicle Books LLC
680 Second Street
San Francisco, California 94107
www.chroniclebooks.com